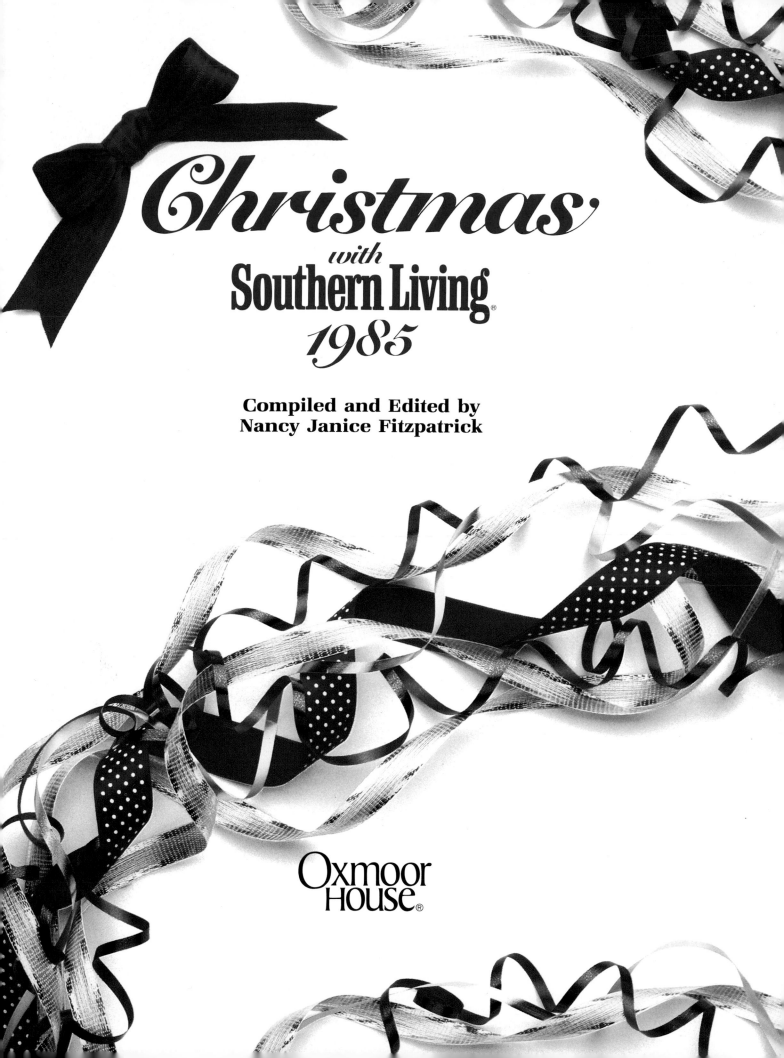

Christmas
with
Southern Living®
1985

**Compiled and Edited by
Nancy Janice Fitzpatrick**

Oxmoor
House®

© 1985 by Oxmoor House, Inc.
Book Division of Southern Progress Corporation
P.O. Box 2463, Birmingham, Alabama 35201

Southern Living® is a federally registered trademark belonging to Southern Living, Inc.

Library of Congress Catalog Card Number: 84-063032
ISBN: 0-8487-0647-1

Manufactured in the United States of America
First Printing

Executive Editor: Candace Conard Bromberg
Production Manager: Jerry Higdon
Art Director: Bob Nance

Christmas with Southern Living 1985
Senior Editor: Nancy Janice Fitzpatrick
Editor: Kathleen English
Assistant Editor: Alison Nichols
Foods Editor: Susan Payne
Editorial Assistant: Lisa Gant
Photography Stylists: Beverly Morrow, Lisa Gant
Pattern Artist: Don K. Smith
Copy Chief: Mary Jean Haddin
Designer: Carol Middleton

Introduction 1

Christmas around the South 3

Christmas at Callaway Gardens 4
Open House in Mississippi 8
Yuletide Traditions at Monticello 14
Hanging of the Greens at Ash Lawn 20
A Storybook Cookie Tree 22

Decorating for the Holidays 25

A Deer Mailbox Cover 26
Make Your Own Natural Wreath 28
   Nature Wreath 28
   Hydrangea Wreath 29
   Magnolia Wreath 30
   Nandina Wreath 31
Rings of Ivy 32
Candles Flicker through
Glass and Glitter 34
Ribbon Plaids 36
Evergreen—The Feeling of Christmas 38

Contents

Scents for Your Kitchen.................................40
   Cinnamon Stick Ornament.........................40
   Potpourri Hot-Dish Mat.............................40
   Potpourri Pillow Wreath...........................42
   Spiced Apple Wreath................................43
Country Gift Baskets....................................44
Just Add a Few Flowers...............................46
Decorate with Your Favorite Things.........48
Featherweight Angel....................................54

Christmas Bazaar 55

Net-Darn a Holiday Backdrop.....................56
Lacy Collars from Old Linens.......................58
Needlepoint Treasures:
Square by Square...60
Ribbon Rays Make a Heavenly Angel........62
Reflections of Home.....................................64
A Rag Doll with Country Style.....................66
Festive Folk Dolls..68
Pom-Poms Make These Sweaters Fun......70
Shadow Appliqué:
Subtle Christmas Color 72
A Basket for the Hearth...............................74
A Cozy, Ribbon-Laced Afghan....................76
Nightshirt Santa...78

Quick! Make Gifts to Have on Hand..........80
   Jar-Lid Toppers.......................................80
   Burlap Bag Wrap.....................................81
   Holly Days Wine Carafe..........................81
Say Welcome with Cross-Stitch...................82

Celebrations from the Kitchen 83

Gather the Family for Holiday Dinner......84
   Fresh Mushroom Soup..............................86
   Stuffed Turkey Breast..............................86
   Oyster Casserole.......................................87
   Sweet Potatoes with Apples.....................87
   Brussels Sprouts with Pecans...................88
   Candied Brandied Cranberries.................88
   Cheesy Bundt Bread.................................88
   Toasted Almond Croquembouche...........89
Christmas Morning Breakfast......................90
   Orange-Spiced Ham..................................90
   Hot Cranberry Compote...........................90
   Honey-Poached Pears...............................92
   Buttermilk Waffles...................................92
   Almond Tea...93
   Orange Tea...93
   South-of-the-Border Hot Chocolate........93

Breads..94
   Chocolate Macaroon Muffins.................94
   Nutty Danish Pastry............................94
   Fresh Lemon Muffins...........................96
   Oatmeal Scones..................................96
   Almond Kringle...................................96
   Caramel Pecan Coffeecake....................97
   Chocolate Applesauce Bread..................97
   Pigs' Ears...98
   Apricot Streusel Gingerbread..................98
   Apricot Brandy Bread...........................99
   Orange Upsidaisies..............................99
Beverages...100
   Viennese Chocolate............................100
   Cranberry Bracer...............................100
   Spicy Tomato Frappé...........................100
   Simple Syllabub.................................102
   Hummers...102
   Hot Apple Rum for Two........................102
   Rum-Cider Tea...................................102
   Cranberry Wine Punch.........................102
Cakes and Pies..103
   Chocolate Mousse Cake.......................103
   Orange Crunch Cake...........................105
   Pumpkin-Brandy Cheesecake.................105
   Peach Preserve Cake...........................106
   Rich Fruitcake....................................106
   Triple Crown Cake..............................107
   Chocolate Cream Pie with
   Cherry Sauce.....................................108
   Sweet Potato Praline Pie.......................109
   Cheddar-Apple Pie..............................109
   French Raisin Pie................................109
Cookies and Candies..................................110
   Vanilla Bean Cookies..........................110
   Ginger Cookies...................................110
   Apricot Granola Bars...........................110
   Mint Chocolate Snaps..........................112
   Chocolate Chip Toffee Grahams.............112
   Lebkuchen Bars..................................112
   White Chocolate Crunch.......................113
   Chocolate Marbles...............................113
   Eggnog Candy.....................................113
   Chocolate Caramels.............................113

Gift Ideas...115
   Spiced Yeast Doughnuts.......................115
   Pickled Dried Apricots.........................115
   Fruited Cranberry Relish.......................115
   Cream Cheese Rounds..........................116
   Moravian Sugar Cake..........................116
   Pineapple-Cherry Sauce........................116
   Cashew-Honey Butter...........................117
   Sangria Jelly......................................117
   Pecans Olé...117
   Carrot Pickles....................................117
Party Fare..118
   Chutney Spread..................................118
   Chicken with Cherry Sauce...................118
   Festive Ham Spread............................120
   Shrimp Dip..120
   Shrimp-Stuffed Cherry Tomatoes............120
   Mini Orange-Glazed Spareribs..............120
   Dried Beef-Cheese Log.........................121
   Baked Gouda in Pastry........................121
   Toasted Mushroom Rolls......................121
   Curried Party Mix...............................122
   Colorful Cheese Ball...........................122
   Pecan Crispies...................................122
   Party Pizzas......................................122

Christmas Journal.................................123

Mailing..124
Gifts and Wishes.......................................125
Size Charts...126
Christmas Card List....................................127
Holiday Calendar.......................................129
Party Planning..134

Patterns..137

Contributors..155

Introduction

What makes a Christmas in the South different from one in other parts of the country? To answer that, you must first define what makes the South unique, and that's not easy. It's not uniform geography or climate; the South is a large and diverse region. Nor is it common history or cultural influences.

Perhaps it lies in the spirit of the people. There's an enormous pride in being a Southerner, a tenacious love of the land, and an unquestionable devotion to home. Much more than just a roof over the head, home is the place of family. And love of family and friends is the ultimate tie that binds a Southern heart.

For most Southerners, there's faith as well—a basic belief that if you treat people right, all will be right. It goes beyond the well-known Southern hospitality. It is an ingrained trust in the goodness of people.

There's also an irrepressible vitality that bubbles from the Southern soul. Southerners have a propensity to get together. They will gather at the drop of a hat for a wedding or funeral with equal enthusiasm.

What, then, does this Southern spirit have to do with Christmas? Everything. Because all these characteristics—love of home and family, belief in people, and joy in getting together—make a Christmas celebration a wondrous experience.

This book provides almost everything you need for a Southern Christmas. However, the most vital ingredient—that unique spirit—is hard to hold on the pages of a book. If you call yourself a Southerner, that's what *you* add—the spirit that will make this the merriest Christmas ever.

Christmas around the South

All across the world, folks come together at Christmastime in reverence and revelry to celebrate their blessings. But nowhere are the festivities more fervent than in the American South. Southerners decorate to the hilt, don their fanciest garb, and open their doors to honor guests. In cozy homes, revered halls, and public parks and institutions, traditions are preserved and exciting new practices introduced.

In "Christmas Around the South," we go visiting—to gain insight into how other Southerners prepare for the holidays. There's a natural curiosity about how other people do things, to compare or contrast their customs with our own.

In Virginia, we view homes of presidents. In Mississippi, we tour a lovely open house. And in Georgia, we're treated to a grand floral display at Callaway Gardens. We also visit a couple who share a charming family tradition with us.

Perhaps you'll see things on these pages that you identify with your own festivities, or discover new ideas to incorporate into this year's decorating. Most certainly, you'll detect some of the elements—including a penchant for pomp and ceremony—that make a Christmas in the South a special occasion.

Christmas at Callaway Gardens

As early as April, the horticulture staff of Callaway Gardens begins nurturing living decorations—especially poinsettias and topiaries—for a holiday extravaganza. Callaway, which is located in Pine Mountain, Georgia, goes all-out to transform the Sibley Horticulture Center into a wonderland for Christmas.

The Sibley Center, opened in 1984, is a five-acre, multi-level, indoor-outdoor greenhouse complex. Constructed of steel and glass, it gives one the illusion of being outside when inside. This beautiful controlled environment, with its 22-foot waterfall cascading over natural rock walls and its seasonal flower displays, is a delight at any time of the year. But shortly after Thanksgiving, it becomes a red, green, and white floral fantasy—with poinsettias galore and life-size topiary animals.

Although the Callaway Christmas flowers include amaryllis, chrysanthemums, coleus, narcissus, azaleas, and primulas, the magical realm of red and green is primarily poinsettias—hundreds of them. The story of how poinsettias became associated with Christmas is a combination of fable and fact. According to legend, the leaves of this native Mexican plant were infused with scarlet color as they lay on the altar, a young girl's humble Christmas Eve offering to the Christ Child. Thus poinsettias became known as *flores de Nochebuena* (Christmas Eve flowers). And the plants' earliest use as Christmas decorations is attributed to Franciscan mission priests in Mexico, who took advantage of the fitting colors and timely blooming season of the plant to use it in nativity processions. The plant that is now so much a part of Christmas decorations in America was introduced here in 1828 by the United States Minister to Mexico, whose name was Joel Roberts Poinsett. The "Christmas Eve flower" was renamed in his honor.

To ensure an abundance of vividly colored poinsettias in full bloom for Christmas, the Callaway gardeners take many measures in the preceding months. The poinsettias are pinched and treated chemically to force branching and to dwarf their growth; otherwise they would become too large and spindly. The plants must experience darkness thirteen hours a day, starting in late September, to bloom nine weeks later. Poinsettias require bright, but not direct, sunlight, and soil must be kept slightly moist at all times. The leaves will drop or turn yellow if the plant is overwatered, becomes too dry, or is exposed to drafts or temperatures exceeding a range of 60°-70° F.

Here's a tip from the professionals. The actual flower of a poinsettia is composed of small buttons. These lie in the center of the colorful (usually red) leaves which are called bracts. Healthy plants have dark green leaves and yellow-green buttons in the center of the bracts. If there are no buttons, the plant has bloomed and may not remain colorful through the holidays.

To maintain your plants, follow the guidelines for care discussed above. With today's improved hardiness for longer lasting blooms and interesting new color varieties, healthy poinsettias should provide cheerful foliage for a month or more.

All the advance preparations to deck the Sibley Center in appropriately colored plant life are just a part of holiday plans at Callaway Gardens. If you'll be traveling through Georgia or are considering a Christmas away from home this year, Callaway is a lovely vacation retreat for the family, just as it was for the family of its textile-industrialist founder Cason Callaway.

Opposite: Over 250 Lady Red poinsettias make up this 20-foot-tall tree. Six-inch pots of dwarfed poinsettias are hung from a metal understructure. A family of topiary deer pause along grassy paths bordered by poinsettias in the Sibley Horticulture Center.

Scheduled special events at Callaway promise a memorable holiday for guests. In addition to tours of the gardens and the year-round recreational activities of fishing, hunting, tennis, and golf (on four scenic courses), there are parties for eggnog sampling and tree trimming, seminars on natural decorations and candle dipping, and live music for dancing and caroling. There are also trips to local craft shops and to nearby points of interest, such as The Little White House, the Georgia home of President Franklin D. Roosevelt. Religious services are held at local churches and in the lovely lakeside Callaway chapel.

Above: These pink-flecked red flowers are from a variety of poinsettia known as Jingle Bells. Callaway gardeners cultivate several varieties, including red, pink, and white ones. The yellow buttons in the center of each blossom are actually the flower. The red leaves that look like a flower are called bracts.

Opposite: The deer shapes are wire forms covered with sphagnum moss. In the spring, creeping fig is planted in the sphagnum moss. By late summer, it is clipped monthly to encourage lush, even coverage. Dieffenbachia leaves are the deer's tails. The antlers are real.

Open House in Mississippi

Members of the New Albany Garden Club feel that the northern part of Mississippi is often overlooked. Coastal areas and the historic Natchez Trace get more publicity and visits from tourists. But people are missing some pretty special territory, according to these 29 women, whose commitment to putting the area on the map begins at home. New Albany, beside the Tallahatchee River in northeast Mississippi, benefits from the garden club's beautification projects.

The club is very active year-round, but especially the first weekend in December, when long-range plans culminate in a fund-raising event for those community projects—an open house or, on alternate years, a tasting tea. In 1984 all hands joined in to produce the natural decorations for the house pictured here. Open to the public for

Above: Candles in the windows and in posted hurricane shades along the drive, and garlands of magnolia leaves on the banisters and around the door, welcome guests to the open house. Designed after The Briars, the antebellum home of Jefferson Davis in Natchez, this house has five dormers.

Above: Here's proof that—with strategic accents of red and green—even a blue room can be decorated for Christmas. Cedar branches with blue berries are tied to bed posts and added to a basket of calico kitties. A star quilt laid at the foot of the bed, and a collection of pillows with holiday sentiments, are a warm welcome to house guests. Possum haw branches fill the blue delft vase beside the bed.

Opposite: Arranged on a beveled mirror table runner, two-foot tapered candles and "iced" branches in glass containers are dramatic decorations with emphasis on height and sparkle. To "ice" branches, spray with white paint and, when dry, with clear shellac. While shellac is still wet, sprinkle with diamond dust from the florist and iridescent glitter from craft shops.

afternoon and evening tours, this fifth biennial open house was attended by over 500 people. (To avoid traffic jams, the club members enlisted their teenaged children to run a shuttle service.)

Although the actual decorating of the house takes place in a flurry of activity the day before the tour, members plan ahead carefully, evaluating the successes and mistakes from previous years. A chairman is appointed, whose tasks are choosing a home and designating committees to be responsible for each room and for the outside of the house. Months in advance, these committees may decide on specific decorations and even begin gathering materials.

The bright orange of bittersweet and Japanese lanterns (in the over-the-mantle boxwood wreath, the tree, and the window wreaths) is a color bridge between the peach walls and the Christmas-red ribbon. It helps tie the unusual color combination together. Other natural materials in these decorations include cedar with blue berries, statice, eucalyptus, holly, small cones, and a cloud of baby's breath for the angel tree topper.

For others considering such an undertaking in their own community, the New Albany group points out that this event, in addition to serving a good cause, is a time to get into the Christmas spirit and to work with friends toward a common goal. As one member puts it, "Working on the open house really gets you in the mood for the holidays. And you always get inspiration for decorating your own home from the creations developed by the group."

Left: This reproduction printer's lantern is topped with grapevines and corkscrew willow branches. To make the pomanders, punch holes all over apples, oranges, lemons, or limes. Insert a wire hanger. Mix ground cinnamon, clove, nutmeg, allspice, grated orange rind, and orrisroot (a natural preservative). Roll fruit in spices, stud with whole cloves, and roll again in spices.

Left: Standing in a butter churn in a kitchen corner, this bare tree is dressed up with red bows, hops from a hornbeam tree, tiny grapevine wreaths trimmed with statice and cones, and fragrant pomanders and bundles of cinnamon sticks. Under the tree, baskets are filled with baked and canned goods, fresh fruit, and place mats—gifts for friends who drop in.

Opposite: Gather miscellaneous objects and fill a big basket to brimming. This antique basket, once used in gathering cotton, overflows with articles of interesting shape, texture, and fragrance.
Tiny pots hold living herbs including mint, thyme, sage, and chives. (Moss and pine bark hide the pots.) Scattered about are apples, oranges, grapes, and nuts; as well as dried materials such as santolina, sliced osage orange, and artemisia. Fantail willow branches shoot up from the center of the arrangement. A wooden reproduction of a horn-blowing whaler, and red candles in terra-cotta holders, complete the imaginative arrangement.

Yuletide Traditions at Monticello

For the community of Charlottesville, Virginia, historic buildings are daily reminders of an important past. In 1982, a series of holiday events called Yuletide Traditions was initiated to salute and preserve that rich heritage. During this annual celebration, time-honored halls are trimmed in period decorations, and people gather there to join in traditional Victorian and early American Christmas customs.

Settled in the 1730s as a tobacco trading center on the Rivanna River, Charlottesville has a number of notable sites for the Yuletide Traditions festivities. For instance, Monticello (shown here), the gracious plantation home of Thomas Jefferson, is decorated inside and out with wreaths, garlands, and centerpieces, all made from plant materials available on the grounds. These decorations—simply elegant and naturally fragrant—are the subject of a how-to workshop. Materials are provided, and the participants can take their decorations home with them.

The most impressive Christmas affairs at Monticello are the evening tours. Illuminated with candles only, Monticello appears much as it might have for a Christmas in the early 1800s. Although building began in 1769, and Jefferson moved into the house in 1772, it was not until 1809 that the structure resembled the house of today. That's because the building of Monticello was a

Right: Luminarias light the path for a candlelight tour of Monticello. Monticello is Italian for "little mountain," significant since most plantations were built beside rivers for transportation of goods. Influenced by European architecture, Jefferson designed this two-story building to appear as one story by joining the windows.

16

Above: In the library, Jefferson amassed 6,000 books, which he sold to the government for the original collection of the Library of Congress. The chair is believed to be the one in which Vice President Jefferson sat when presiding over the U.S. Senate.

Right: Thomas Jefferson was trained as a lawyer. He became the author of the Declaration of Independence, *a governor of Virginia, a secretary of state, a vice-president, and the third president of the United States.*

Left: Step into the entrance hall at Monticello, and the balcony railing—symmetrically draped with wreaths and garlands of natural materials—captures your attention. Materials include boxwood, pine, deodara cones, apples, Queen Anne's lace, yarrow, glycerinized magnolia leaves, sycamore and sweetgum balls, and cedrela pods. Overhead is one of the friezes that Jefferson derived from Roman architecture.

Above: The centerpieces for the dining room table are trees shaped from cedar and apples with pomegranate tree toppers. This room is painted blue to match the Wedgwood medallions above the mantel. Hidden inside the right side of the fireplace is a dumbwaiter, which brought wine up from the cellar below.

hobby to Thomas Jefferson. He took much satisfaction in the construction process. The result—this dignified Greco-Roman-style structure—is evidence of Jefferson's diverse talents.

Another site of Yuletide Traditions is the University of Virginia, founded in 1819, which hosts several concerts, including madrigal singers presenting rounds, catches, and carols. And in the historic district of downtown Charlottesville, there is a

children's Victorian Christmas party. At the Michie Tavern, an authentic 18th-century pub which today is a museum and restaurant, lavish banquets are served in the style of Old Virginia—with country ham, roast turkey, and plenty of stuffings. Live dulcimer music is played in the background. And at Ash Lawn (pictured on the following pages), the home of Thomas Jefferson's friend, James Monroe, the ceremonial hanging of the greens begins the festivities.

18

Above: The narrow mantels at Monticello require simple decorations. These are notable for their carefully selected materials, which complement the decor. The color of the Wedgwood mantel medallions in the dining room is delicately echoed in the pale blue of cedar berries. And the dainty anemones (Japanese wildflowers) are as graceful as the dancing maidens.

Right: In a bedroom, this mantel arrangement of fir interspersed with Queen Anne's lace coordinates with the wallpaper—the only wallpaper in the house.

19

Top left: During the Victorian family Christmas party, adults and children make period ornaments for the tree trimming. In years past, lace fans, pomanders, sachets, and tussie-mussies have been assembled. This year cornucopias, bead ornaments, and strings of cranberries and popcorn were made. Cookie cutter cutouts were the favorites of the preschoolers.

Above left: Ash Lawn, a typical farmhouse of the 1800s, is surrounded by boxwoods. The semicircular window decorations are made from boxwood clippings, berries, and red and yellow apples attached to wire mesh covering a wooden frame.

Above right: These festively dressed double-decked doors greet visitors to Ash Lawn. Boxwood and fruit decorations are stand-out trimmings against the yellow frame house.

Hanging of the Greens at Ash Lawn

In November, 1799, the James Monroe family returned from France in time for Christmas in their new Virginia home. During Monroe's service as minister to France, his friend and mentor, Thomas Jefferson, had supervised the construction of Ash Lawn. Today Ash Lawn is preserved in honor of Monroe, who lived there 25 years and called it his "cabin-castle."

Monroe held more public offices than any other president. He served as governor and senator of Virginia; secretary of state and of war simultaneously; minister to France, England, and Spain; and fifth president of the United States. He is especially remembered for the Monroe Doctrine, his statement of foreign policy warning European governments not to intervene in American affairs.

Open to the public, Ash Lawn is located on 550 acres and retains the atmosphere of a working farm. As part of the nearby Charlottesville community's Yuletide Traditions, Ash Lawn hosts a variety of holiday celebrations. For instance, visitors are welcome to cut their own Christmas trees from the wooded lands. (There is no charge, but a donation is requested.) Another activity is the hanging of the greens, colorful boxwood and fruit decorations, on the yellow frame farmhouse.

Special nights at Ash Lawn include a presentation of Christmas customs, decorations, and music from the years of Monroe's presidency (1817-1825) through Queen Victoria's reign (1837-1901). This is a candlelight affair with guides dressed in period costume conducting the festivities. But the most popular event at Ash Lawn is the Victorian family Christmas, an evening of caroling around the piano, homemade refreshments, ornament making, tree trimming, and the lighting of the Yule log.

Above: Monroe's two daughters, one of whom had the first White House wedding, slept here as children. Furniture from the house was sold years ago due to debt. But many original pieces have been acquired to restore Ash Lawn. Most other furnishings are of the period and are representative of the time the Monroes lived there. The crib in this bedroom actually belonged to the family. The dolls probably date to the time of Monroe's grandchildren.

A Storybook Cookie Tree

Once upon a time, there was a young family—a mother, a father, and three little boys. Each year at Christmastime, they made cookies together. They mixed gingerbread dough, rolled it out, stamped shapes with cookie cutters, and decorated the baked cookies with colored frosting.

One Christmas, when the boys were four, five, and six years old, they wanted to make cookies in the shape of their favorite storybook hero—Pegasus. Since they could find no cookie cutter for him, the father decided to try his hand at making one. He sketched the design on paper, and with pliers, bent metal strips into intricate shapes. His successful result—the flying horse—was the family's first homemade cutter.

In the following years, the mother's passion for children's literature, and her growing collection of storybooks, inspired ideas for new cutters. With the exception of such notables as Snoopy and Woodstock from the comic strips, and Kermit the Frog of television fame, the 136 cutter characters are from fairy tales, fables, mythology, bedtime stories, and poems.

In some cases, characters from a single story come together on the display tree—a branch sprayed with gold paint. (For instance, the cast of *The House at Pooh Corner*—Pooh, Christopher Robin, Piglet, and Tigger—meet on the tree each year.) Although many shapes were drawn freehand, some are interpretations of works by well-known illustrators such as 19th-century artist John Tenniel (*Alice in Wonderland*), and contemporary illustrator Maurice Sendak (*Where the Wild Things Are*).

That first family cookie making was over thirty years ago. The boys are grown now, with families of their own. Three years ago, the couple, now retired, moved from Connecticut to Georgia. In their new community, they decided that their unusual

Above: With the voice of experience, the Cookie Man notes that, "Some characters make good cutters, and some don't." To try out a shape, he first cuts a cardboard template, and then cuts the dough out around it. If, after baking and decorating, the design is satisfactory, he proceeds to make a cutter by shaping metal strips with pliers to match the curves of the pattern. He solders the ends of the strip together. For reinforcement, he solders wire between detailed areas. Finally, he files the rough edges. As a surgeon, his skilled hands are perfect for this detailed work.

Top: At last count, there were 136 storybook cutters. When not in use, they snuggle together on a pegboard under the kitchen cabinets like a giant jigsaw puzzle.

Look closely to identify famous storybook characters masquerading as cookies. There are Raggedy Ann and Andy; the Gingham Dog and the Calico Cat; Mole and Mr. Badger from The Wind in the Willows; *the Cat and the Fiddle, the Cow and the Moon, and the Dish and the Spoon from "Hey, Diddle, Diddle"; the Trumpeter Swan; Cinderella's coach; the Cat in the Hat; Paddington Bear; the Little Engine that Could; the Balloon that sailed* Around the World in 80 Days; *the Owl and the Pussycat; and even the Grinch who stole Christmas, among many others. Pegasus, the flying horse made from the family's first cookie cutter, always has a place of prominence at the top of the tree.*

Christmas tradition might be a good way to make friends. Word spread about the storybook tree, and people called or dropped by for a look. The family presented each new acquaintance with a storybook cookie. (Many children came to know the couple simply as the Cookie Man and the Cookie Lady.)

After all the cookies are baked and have cooled on racks, the decorating begins. Many colors of frosting are prepared, and favorite color patterns (assembled in a notebook over the years) are followed for each special design. Large color areas are covered with glaze frosting, and details are added with tube frosting. For the tiniest details, toothpicks are used to apply the frosting.

Interest in the cookies has snowballed. Last year, the cookie couple made 800 cookies. Most of these were handed out to visitors. One of each storybook character—175 cookies in all— went on the tree. (There are more characters than cutters because—as with the bunny quartet, Flopsy, Mopsy, Cottontail, and Peter—the same cutter is used for several characters.)

The cookie makers had a new, and especially Southern, experience this past Christmas. Cookies started tumbling from the tree as a result of an unusually warm December and an inevitable element of this region's climate—humidity. The solution? The couple turned on the air-conditioner and met shirt-sleeved guests at the door with extra cardigans!

For their annual cookie celebration, the couple begin the weekend after Thanksgiving by making a 20-pound batch of gingerbread cookie dough. After about four days of rolling, stamping, and baking the cookies, they spread them out on racks for decorating, filling every available kitchen surface and even spilling over into the dining room. As they mix frosting and try to find all the cookies that need that color, urgent calls ring out: "Who needs red?" or "I need some blue over here!"

The couple package these colorful creations so that they can be seen and people can pick their favorite to take home. They place a cookie character, or two to three from one story, in a plastic tray (the kind butchers use), wrap it in plastic wrap, and add a ribbon. As the Cookie Lady has observed, "The children take a little while to choose their favorite cookie, the teenaged girls take a long time, and the grandmothers take forever. The grannies invariably get to the door, change their minds, and come back for another look."

It's a bit of work to prepare so many detailed cookie characters each year, but the anticipation of seeing old and new friends makes it all worthwhile. And the house is filled with the warm, spicy fragrance of gingerbread for days.

Decorating for the Holidays

In the late fall, when it's time to bring out the Christmas boxes, you not only unpack treasures collected through the years. You release a torrent of memories. So many of the items have a story and meaning. And how you choose to interpret the holidays through your decorations is a highly personal matter.

This time, look for new settings or new ways to arrange the cherished decorations from years past. Then flip through this section for delightful additions. Perhaps you could try a creative arrangement with a prized collection. Spicy wreaths and dish mats in the kitchen emit a delicious fragrance. And something as simple as candles flickering in glittering holders casts an overlay of golden light on an embellished room.

Decorate from nature by gathering favorite Southern materials—nandina berries, hydrangea blossoms, magnolia leaves, and greenery. Wreaths woven from flowers can bedeck doorways, ring candles, and float on mirrors. Just the right spot of red in a floral arrangement carries Christmas into dining areas. Evergreen flowing over furniture and down banisters brings both the sight and scent of the season indoors.

Use the ideas in this chapter as they are or allow them to spark your creativity as you adorn your home this year.

A Deer Mailbox Cover

Who could doubt that Santa will receive that special letter when it's mailed from a reindeer mailbox? Sporting a wreath in place of the traditional sleigh collar, this merry mailbox cover extends the season's greetings to passersby, at the same time he's collecting your cards and correspondence. The reindeer cover is designed to be custom-fitted to your mailbox and to slip on and off easily for years of holiday use.

MATERIALS (for standard-size mailbox):
  patterns on page 154
  17 (1½" x 28") ¼" wooden slats
  8 feet (1" x 12") wood
  band saw or jigsaw
  C clamps
  1 (9" x 13") piece ½" plywood
  drill with ¼" bit
  2 (¼" x 2") wood screws
  wood glue
  nails
  hammer
  rasp (a wood-cutting file to shape reindeer head and antlers)
  sandpaper
  one 4"-length of ¼" wood doweling
  brown spray paint
  light brown acrylic paint
  artist's brush

From the 1" x 12" wood cut the following:
  4 (7" x 12") pieces for reindeer head—length on grain of wood
  1 (12" x 20") piece for antlers
  1 (4" x 6") piece for tail
  2 (9" x 10") pieces for ends
For reindeer head, glue and stack the four 7" x 12" pieces. Clamp with C clamps and let dry. Trace the flag on your mailbox. Transfer the flag pattern to the plywood, and cut it out. Sand the flag and drill a ¼" hole through the staff.

Transfer antlers pattern to the 12" x 20" piece and cut out. Drill a 1" hole in the bottom center of antlers and sand smooth. Transfer tail pattern to the 4" x 6" piece and cut out. Trace the end of your mailbox, and add 1¼" to all sides. Cut the rear end piece from one 9" x 10" piece of wood. For the front end piece, glue the other 9" x 10" piece to the plywood piece, trim excess plywood and clamp with C clamps. After the glue has dried, cut to the same size as rear end piece.

To allow for opening the mailbox door, make a pattern by tracing the door and adding ¼" to the top and sides. Center, transfer to front end piece, and cut through entire piece. (Begin at bottom edge and cut an arch.) To assemble the body frame, measure length of mailbox, and position front end piece (plywood side facing rear) and rear end piece that distance apart. Nail the slats around the front end piece flush with the front edge. Then nail the slats to the rear end piece. (Slats will extend several inches beyond edge.)

Remove the C clamps from the four 7" x 12" pieces. Transfer reindeer head pattern to wood, and use band saw to cut out. Drill a 3" hole in top center of reindeer head. Round the edges of head with rasp and sand smooth. Place head on body frame and nail from the underside to secure. Apply glue to one end of dowel and insert it into head. Let dry. Place antlers on dowel.

To shape rear end of reindeer, measure 1½" from rear piece along bottom slat. Draw a diagonal line from this point to the top corner of the sixth slat above, and saw along this line. Repeat for other side.

Spray-paint body, head, tail, and antlers brown. With light brown paint and a brush, add eyes, nose, and shading to bottom slats. To attach flag, drill a hole near front edge of fourth slat from bottom of frame and insert a wood screw through flag into frame. Insert a second wood screw into frame 4" up from flag base to hold flag in place when not in use. To attach tail, insert cut-out slot into middle rear slat. If desired, place a small wreath or bow around reindeer neck.

Make Your Own Natural Wreath

As if strolling through the woods on a winter's day weren't its own reward, you can use such an outing to harvest materials for one of the exquisite wreaths on these pages.

Wreaths can decorate more than walls and doors, as you see above. This wreath, made from wild oak-leaf hydrangeas, encircles a three-wicked candle to form a focal point on a prized antique table.

Wait to cut hydrangeas until their color is beginning to fade. If you'd like them to become golden brown, treat them with glycerine as described below, or hang them upside down for one week to dry naturally.

(The soft color seen here came from a careful coating of spray paint.) When they're ready, cut the stems close to the blooms, and use U-shaped florist's pins to attach the flowers to a straw or craft-foam wreath form.

Natural elements make striking wreaths when used alone, as is the case with the hydrangea wreath above. If, however, you like to mix natural elements as an artist combines paints on canvas, consider the wreath opposite.

Broomweed, various grasses, hydrangea, and baby's breath lay the groundwork for decorative elements like seedpods, slices of

pinecones, and loops of braided jute. Combine your area's native plants, and you can achieve the same beautiful intricacy. All that remains is to choose silk flowers, like the tiger lilies here, and a coordinating bow, for the desired accent color.

Nandina berries gracefully spin around a wire form in the wreath opposite. Just use florist's picks with wires and clear filament or fishing line to attach nandina clusters. The tips of one cluster cover the ends of another, giving an unbroken line of berries.

Gold magnolia leaves glisten in the wreath above. To keep leaves pliable, condition them in a glycerine solution before gilding them. First take cuttings of magnolia branches and, at the end of each stem, make a couple of 3-inch-long cuts lengthwise. Then place branches in a large container filled with a mixture of three parts water to one part glycerine. Keep adding the mixture as it evaporates, and after about two months, leaves should be a rich brown color.

At this point, the leaves are ready to be removed from the branches and sprayed with gold paint. When the paint is dry, use florist's picks with wires to attach the leaves to a straw wreath form. Anchor wreath with a plaid bow in matching colors.

Rings of Ivy

Graceful and growing, a living ivy wreath provides a splendid and practical alternative to decorating with flowers. If started a month or two before the holidays, the ivy wreath will have sufficient time to grow into a thriving decoration for you or a friend.

Clip several long pieces of ivy and let them soak overnight in a bucket of water. Then choose a container with adequate drainage, fill with soil, and root the ivy. For added versatility, use a plastic or clay container that may be placed inside a decorative one. Use a wire wreath form anchored in the soil with bent coat hangers, or make a wreath form using #18 florist's wire.

Starting from either side of the wire form, carefully wrap one end of ivy around and through the layers of wire, leaving the other end rooted in the soil. Continue this process with all the rooted clippings. Water often and, as ivy grows, trim it to follow the shape and to fill in the gaps of the wire form.

When ready to use as an arrangement, place the plastic container inside a decorative one, filling in any extra space with sphagnum moss to keep in moisture.

Candles Flicker through Glass and Glitter

Candle holders sprinkled with diamond dust splinter candlelight into fiery facets. Glue a design and diamond dust to glass, light a candle, and watch the magic unfold.

MATERIALS:
  **clear glass candle holders or
    hurricane lamp chimneys
  paper napkins with holiday motifs
  clear-drying craft glue
  1″ paint brush or poly (sponge) brush
  diamond dust**

Choose napkins with white backgrounds. Separate the layer with the design from the rest of the napkin, and cut the design out. (Don't worry if you leave a little white paper around the edges. Glue and diamond dust will cover it.) Cover your work surface with newspapers.

Paint a thin coat of glue on glass over an area slightly larger than design. Place design on the glued area and gently press in place. Apply a thin coat of glue over the design and on the part of the glass surface you want to cover with diamond dust. Quickly sprinkle diamond dust on glued surface. Shake excess onto paper (save it for reuse), and allow glue to dry thoroughly.

Ribbon Plaids

Try ruffled and plaid accents that complement your furnishings to set the right tone for Christmas. The ribbon-appliquéd pillows and table cover shown here accessorize the plaid couch and the priscillas hanging in the bay window. Arrange ribbon in a plaid pattern on fabric, and experiment with a dramatically asymmetrical arrangement. Muslin is used here, but choose any plain inexpensive fabric.

PILLOW

MATERIALS:
  ½ yard (45″-wide) muslin or similar cotton fabric
  red, green, and gold ribbon (for plaid design) in assorted widths
  black cording
  24 oz. fiberfill

Prewash fabric and ribbon. Cut two 14″ squares from fabric. With pencil or chalk, lightly mark design on fabric (front of pillow). Appliqué different widths of ribbon in one direction and outline with black cording. Continue this process in several different directions, allowing the ribbon groups to intersect and overlap.

Place pillow front on pillow back (right sides together). Using a ¼″ seam allowance, machine-stitch edges together, leaving one side open. Turn pillow right side out and stuff with fiberfill. Slip-stitch closed.

WREATH

MATERIALS:
  1 yard (45″-wide) muslin or similar cotton fabric
  3⅓ yards picot ribbon (for ruffle)
  red, green, and gold ribbon (for plaid design) in assorted widths
  12 oz. package of fiberfill

Prewash the fabric and the ribbon. Cut two 14″ squares from the fabric. With pencil or chalk, lightly mark the plaid design on one square (front of pillow), and pin the ribbon in place. Appliqué the ribbon to make the plaid design.

On plain square of fabric, center and draw circle as large as fabric allows. Draw a 4″ diameter center circle. Cut out both circles. Use this as a pattern for cutting wreath top from fabric with design.

To make ruffle, cut three 5″ x 40″ strips and sew short ends together to make a long strip. Fold in half lengthwise, right sides out, and iron. Machine-stitch decorative ribbon ⅛″ from folded edge. Gather raw edges, pin and baste (right sides together) to front of wreath, matching raw edges.

Place wreath back on wreath front (right sides together) and, using a ½″ seam allowance, machine-stitch.

Using ½″ seam allowance, machine-stitch the inner circle, leaving a 4″ opening for stuffing. Turn the wreath right side out. Stuff the wreath with fiberfill and slip-stitch the opening closed.

TABLECLOTH

MATERIALS:
  muslin or similar cotton fabric
  red, green, and gold ribbon (for plaid design) in assorted widths

Prewash fabric and ribbon. Measure size of table to be covered, and cut desired shape and size from fabric. Turn raw edges ¼″ to right side and iron. Cover raw edges with band of ribbon and machine-stitch close to edge, mitering ribbon at corners to give a finished edge.

Determine area to be covered by plaid design. With pencil or chalk, lightly mark design on fabric. Cut ribbon strips to corresponding lengths, pin in place, and appliqué to make the plaid design. Conceal raw edges of plaid design with ribbon border, mitering ribbon at corners.

Evergreen—
The Feeling
of Christmas

Thousands of years before the Christmas tree made its appearance in American Christmas celebrations, the evergreen was a symbol of long life and immortality. The Romans exchanged evergreens as tokens of good wishes, and primitive tribes believed evergreens could ward off evil spirits. Today, by decorating with these fresh and living ornaments, we tap the ancient belief in the rebirth and renewal of life.

Whether your decorations reflect a symbolic belief or simply an admiration of nature, "hanging the greens" is an enjoyable Christmas tradition. Use greenery that is native to your area to get the freshest cuttings and to reduce cost. Cut greenery above a new bud so that the spring growth can fill in where you cut. Pine and juniper can stand a liberal clipping, while boxwood and holly should be clipped only slightly during the winter months. Leave clippings in a bucket of water overnight in a garage or cool basement. Dip holly, pine, and cedar in candle wax to seal resin. (Pine and cedar should not be placed against painted walls because their resin may stain.)

Boxwood and Douglas fir are good choices for garlands. Cut the branches into workable-size sprigs. With all cuttings arranged in the same direction, wrap several sprigs together with florist's wire to form small bunches, and tie to a rope base with florist's wire. A green rope base (dyed or spray-painted) requires less greenery. To add a bow, insert florist's wire through center and wrap wire around garland.

Hang the finished garland from small nails in beams or walls, or suspend it from the ceiling with nylon fishing line and thumbtacks. To protect a banister from resin, wrap banister with inexpensive ribbon before draping garland. (Clean resin from hands with vegetable oil.)

39

Scents for Your Kitchen

Spice up your kitchen with aromatic decorations. An ornament of stacked cinnamon sticks, a mat for hot dishes with a pocket of potpourri, a wreath of potpourri-puffed pillows, or a spicy apple wreath will send festive fragrances wafting through the air.

CINNAMON STICK ORNAMENT

MATERIALS:
8-10 cinnamon sticks
1 yard (¼"-wide) red ribbon
craft glue
red bow to match ribbon

Break the cinnamon sticks into 2"-3" pieces. Holding both ends of the ribbon, place a cinnamon piece in center of ribbon and tie around cinnamon piece. If needed, add a small dab of glue between cinnamon stick and ribbon to hold. Cross next cinnamon piece on top of previous piece, and tie with ribbon. Continue this process, using all cinnamon stick pieces. Tie knot in top of ribbon to hold pieces securely. Add a bow to the top of ornament to decorate and conceal knot.

POTPOURRI HOT-DISH MAT

MATERIALS:
patterns on page 149
½ yard (45"-wide) green Christmas print fabric
scraps of assorted Christmas fabrics (white and red)
13" square extra-thick polyester batting
¼ yard muslin fabric
1 cup potpourri

Transfer patterns to fabrics and cut out: 8 green print triangles, 4 red triangles, 4 white triangles, 4 white squares, and 1 green print square. From the green Christmas print fabric, cut 2 each of the following:
3¼" x 8½" borders
3¼" x 13" borders
8" x 13¼" back pieces
Following Figure (page 149), sew together all pieces for the center design. Iron the seams toward the darker fabric. Using a ½" seam allowance, sew the shorter borders to opposite sides of design. Follow the same procedure for the longer borders. Iron the seams toward the borders. Sew batting to the wrong side of the square along edges, using a ½" seam allowance. Trim excess batting from the seam.

Using a ½" seam allowance, finish one long edge of each back piece. Overlap the finished edges 1¾" and pin together. (Do not sew together). Pin design to back pieces, wrong sides together, and stitch all sides, using a ½" seam allowance. Clip corners and turn. Stitch along seam joining quilt block and border. (This forms the pocket on the back side.)

From the muslin, cut 2 (7") squares. Using a ½" seam allowance, sew together three sides. Fill with one cup potpourri and finish sewing edge. Insert muslin square in back pocket of hot pad. If desired, make a loop for hanging.

POTPOURRI PILLOW WREATH

MATERIALS:
   pattern on page 149
   clear acetate (for stencil)
   craft knife
   1 yard (45″-wide) muslin
   red and green acrylic paint
   stencil brush
   1 cup potpourri
   12 oz. bag fiberfill
   6½ yards (¼″-wide) red ribbon
   12″ wire wreath form

Tape acetate over pattern and cut along lines. Cut muslin into 24 (6″) squares. Using paints, stencil the holly design on 8 muslin squares as shown on pattern. Let paint dry thoroughly.

Fold each square in half with right sides together, and stitch open edges, leaving a 2″ opening on the long side. Trim corners and turn. Mix fiberfill and potpourri together and stuff squares. Slip-stitch closed.

Cut 24 (8″) pieces of ribbon. Place the ribbon in the center of the pillow and tie it to the wreath form. Tie the stenciled pillows to front center and use the plain pillows to fill out the wreath.

SPICED APPLE WREATH

MATERIALS:
   apples
   ground cinnamon
   clove pieces
   hot glue gun
   vine wreath
   twigs

With apple stem up, cut apples in ¼″-wide slices (see photograph). Dip apple slice in cinnamon and stud with cloves, covering both sides of slice.

Apply hot glue to slice and glue slice to wreath form. Glue a green leaf to each side of apple slice. If desired, accent the apple slice wreath with greenery or ribbon.

Country Gift Baskets

For the charm of a country Christmas, stencil chipwood baskets with meaningful symbols—hearts of love, pineapples for hospitality, and stars for goodwill. For a gift, enclose fruit or homemade preserves to round out your country style.

MATERIALS:
   patterns on page 148
   chipwood market baskets in various
      shapes and sizes
   acrylic paints (camel, ivy green, red
      clay, indigo, and slate blue)
   disposable aluminum pan (for mixing
      stain)
   sponge
   newspapers
   masking tape
   craft knife
   stencil brush or pieces of sponge
      (one for each color)
   artist's brushes

Baskets should be stained before being stenciled or painted. To stain baskets, mix 3 parts water to 1 part paint in the disposable aluminum pan. Roll the basket in the mixture, using the sponge to ensure that all areas are covered with stain. Shake the basket and wipe off excess stain. Place on newspapers and let dry thoroughly.

Paint basket handles and rims first (see photograph), and let dry. Basket designs may be painted freehand or stenciled. To make stencil, place acetate over pattern and tape to secure. On a protected surface, cut acetate along pattern lines. For details too small to be stenciled, paint freehand after stenciled design has dried.

Lightly pencil a guideline to keep stencils straight. Tape stencil to basket. Paint surface using an up-and-down motion. (See pattern for color schemes.) Each time stencil is removed, wipe clean with a damp rag. Use artist's brush to add details.

44

Just Add a Few Flowers

Three simple daisies form red accents in greenery, taking the flower arrangement at left from everyday to holiday. Gerbera daisies sit in a nest of variegated holly, pine, and cedar. The holly's highlighted leaves provide definition within the greenery, and its berries repeat the flowers' blaze of color. A pinecone gives the look of patterned weight at the base of the arrangement, while cedar softly drapes over the sides of a country-style basket. And the various elements are balanced by the height, contrasting color, and texture of cinnamon sticks.

This arrangement is subtle enough to work in almost any room's decor, as you can see from the way it complements the collection of majolica ware in the Welsh cupboard and the majolica candlesticks flanking the bountiful basket. The greenery will probably outlast the flowers, but you can extend the life of the arrangement by purchasing a few fresh flowers to replace the withered ones as needed.

Have you ever tried fruit and vegetables in a flower arrangement? In the arrangement above, purple kale adds depth and interest within pine branches. A bunch of grapes is draped along the curve of the vine basket's handle, adding grace to the arrangement with its pale green color and off-center placement. The deep kale and light grapes are ideal foils for brilliant red gerbera and chrysanthemum daisies and tulips. And the spiked rays of the flowers are interestingly echoed in the spiny metal leaves of the pineapple candlesticks.

Decorate with Your Favorite Things

Collections, though sometimes amassed for their value, are even more often gathered for sentimental reasons. These treasured objects express your personality and style. What better elements could you find to create one-of-a-kind decorations?

Perhaps you have a collection that lends itself to being shaped into a configuration of the season. Try attaching individual elements to a wreath or tree form as shown at right. The tree is covered with an assortment of colorful trinkets—baubles, prizes of the gum-ball machine variety, miniature toys, even political memorabilia. Overflowing from the tree are tiny treasures, including several Santas. Or add elements associated with the holidays to your collection—such as greenery, bells, ribbons, tiny lights, even cookies. Below, a string of gingerbread boys are hung from a glass-front cabinet that is filled with keepsakes, drawing new attention to a year-round display. (The china doll heads are over 70 years old.)

If a collection includes figures of animals or people, as in the grouping on page 50, let

The Night Before Christ[mas]

By Clement Clarke Moore

'TWAS the night before Christmas,
When all through the house
Not a creature was stirring, not even a mouse.
The stockings were hung by the chimney with care,
In hopes that St. Nicholas soon would be there.
The children were nestled all snug in their beds,
While visions of sugar-plums danced in their heads.
And Mamma in her kerchief, and I in my cap,
Had just settled our brains for a long winter's nap.
When out on the lawn there arose such a clatter,
I sprang from my bed to see what was the matter.
Away to the window I flew like a flash,
Tore open the shutters and threw up the sash.
The moon, on the breast of the new-fallen snow,
Gave a lustre of mid-day to objects below.
When, what to my wondering eyes should appear,
But a miniature sleigh, and eight tiny reindeer.

And then in a twinkling I heard on the roof
The prancing and pawing of each little hoof.
As I drew in my head, and was turning around,
Down the chimney St. Nicholas came with a bound.
He was dressed all in fur from his head to his foot,
And his clothes were all tarnished with ashes and soot.
A bundle of toys he had flung on his back,
And he looked like a peddler just opening his pack.
His eyes how they twinkled! his dimples how merry!
His cheeks were like roses, his nose like a cherry.
His droll little mouth was drawn up like a bow,
And the beard on his chin was as white as the snow.
The stump of a pipe he held tight in his teeth,
And the smoke it encircled his head like a wreath.
He had a broad face and a little round belly,
That shook, when he laughed, like a bowl full of jelly.
He was chubby and plump — a right jolly old elf.

them take part in the festivities by playing significant roles. The appealing composition shown contains an evergreen wreath decorated with clove-studded pomanders, cinnamon sticks, and lichens. Hung close to the tabletop, it serves as a backdrop for a tableau of a music maker and some antique animals, which assume the roles of Noah's chosen ones when placed around a folk-painted ark.

At left, Christmas cards are displayed in a hutch, propped amidst a collection of blue-and-white china. This is another example of how seasonal trimmings can command refreshed awareness and appreciation for everyday displays. (Notice the greenery and seedpod arrangement on top of the cabinet. Don't miss the opportunity to decorate surprising places—over doors, windowsills, wherever—in your home.)

On the table is a collection of colorful rag dolls, souvenirs of the country's bicentennial celebration. The dolls lean against an antique knife box filled with boxwood greenery and bright red apples. And because this arrangement is low and therefore unobtrusive to across-the-table conversation (something to consider with centerpieces), these dolls can provide cheerful company even at mealtime.

At right, a family of teddy bears gather for a picnic complete with a tiny china tea set. On the door behind the table, bear cookies frolic on a wreath of vines, echoing the teddy bear theme. So few elements, yet with this inventive setting—a tabletop vignette—they convey a lot of charm.

Look around your house for the things you cherish. Even if you don't have a formal collection, you may want to bring some of your favorite things forward to be accented at holiday time. Consider how you might present them for unique decorations. The displays shown here—some whimsical, some pretty, all unusual and interesting—illustrate how a few of your favorite things, arranged with ingenuity, can capture the joy of the season in your own very personal, individual style.

Featherweight Angel

This airy angel springs from balsa wood, paint, and yarn. Let her carry your Christmas tidings atop a gift or your tree.

MATERIALS:
    patterns on page 148
    balsa wood
    jigsaw
    fine sandpaper or emery board
    acrylic paints (black, pink, red, and
      blue)
    artist's brush
    acrylic paint sealer (optional)
    ¼″ brass screw eye
    12″ twisted loop yarn
    craft glue

Transfer pattern to wood. Cut out in one piece using a jigsaw. Gently sand off any rough spots around edges.

Paint angel following photograph, leaving one segment in each heart the natural color of the wood to match the wings. After painting, spray with acrylic sealer, for a shiny finish, or leave natural.

Attach a small screw eye to top center of head for hanging. Using the 12″ piece of yarn, glue one end to back of head behind the screw eye. Glue yarn across one side of face, around to the other side of the face, crossing over the first line of yarn at forehead. Continue wrapping head until it is covered.

Christmas Bazaar

An extra chill in the wind prompts you to add another log to the fire. Children begin to clean their rooms without the usual reminders. Perhaps a younger child asks you how many *s*'s are in "unicycle." The realization comes slowly—Christmas is definitely on the way!

Think ahead. Those weeks before Christmas are always bustling with neighbors dropping by, visiting relatives, or children returning home. Time is so precious that preparations can never begin too soon. This year, why not start now? Avoid the rush and crush of the shopping crowds and opt for Christmas in your own style. Use the time you have now to create thoughtful gifts with special touches of your own, and begin a new legacy of gift giving.

"Christmas Bazaar" offers you an abundance of gift possibilities. This section combines popular techniques with new ideas, all with complete patterns and instructions—in a range of skill areas. For instance, a simple punching technique turns soft sheet copper into glowing ornaments. And a special fabric that hardens after molding can make an ordinary basket into a pretty hearth basket. The needlework techniques in this chapter run from a few quick and easy stitches—such as pom-pom designs sewn onto purchased sweaters—to an exquisite needlepoint Christmas stocking with matching ornaments. Strands of ribbon stitched to a moiré background produce a radiant angel. And a simply cut wooden Santa gives a unique perspective of the kind old gentleman.

Should you need a last-minute gift for the mailman or a favorite teacher, don't worry. In this chapter, ideas abound for extra gifts to have on hand.

Net-Darn a Holiday Backdrop

Suspend this lacy panel in a window; then watch as it gently diffuses wintertime sunlight or glimmers in the evening with reflected candlelight.

Dove and Christmas tree motifs are created by net darning, a modern variation on the intricate art of filet lace making. The technique is quick: Cotton thread is simply woven through net. A dowel slips in the top for easy hanging and in the bottom to keep the net smooth. Grace an entire room with these delicate panels, or make one for someone with a taste for the romantic.

MATERIALS:
    charts on page 142
    21″ x 39″ white net (126 x 234
       squares, 6 squares per inch)
    120 yards #3 mercerized white
       cotton thread
    #16 tapestry needle
    2 (17″-long) ⅜″ dowels
    1″ screw picture hook
    colored thread (any color)

Choose net that will not shrink or require a hoop, if possible. If not, wash and block net before beginning.

Being careful to leave the correct number of squares, remove the selvage (finished edge) from net. Turn under 6 squares on a long side for hem. Leaving a 3″ tail of thread, darn through both thicknesses in last row of squares until row is filled—about 4 threads. (Figure 1.) Knot and trim excess thread. Repeat for other long side.

Fold under 12 squares on top and bottom and stitch as for sides. These openings form casings for the dowels.

Using colored thread, section net into 3 panels. (Figure 2.) Position doves in top panel according to chart and begin darning at left dove's head. Darn horizontally and move downward diagonally, being careful not to fill in open squares. (Figure 3.)

To finish unconnected areas of design, weave ¾″ of thread vertically through stitches on back and cut excess close to net.

Repeat technique for tree in center panel and doves in bottom panel. Following chart, darn snowflakes. Leaving colored thread until it's no longer needed as a guide, darn borders as shown on chart.

Sand dowels and insert in casings. Screw picture hook into center of top dowel.

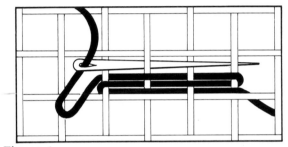

Figure 1
Weave back and forth until row is filled.

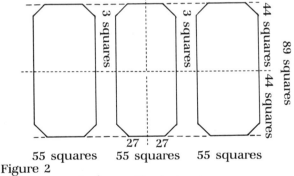

Figure 2
Measurements for sectioning net

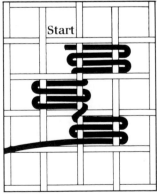

Figure 3
When working downward, darn diagonally and wrap thread around corners as shown here.

58

Lacy Collars from Old Linens

Frame a pretty face with a frilly collar, and be prepared for second glances. Old linens from the family trunk or local flea market convert easily into detachable, lacy collars. (Just make sure, before you start to alter it, that you don't prefer the linen in its original form.)

LINED COLLAR

MATERIALS:

    pattern on page 148
    lacy piece of linen or doily
    contrasting fabric for lining (twice
       the size of linen piece)
    thread to match linen and fabric
    hook and eye

Make patterns as for unlined collar. Fold linen in half, wrong side out, and crease along fold. Use patterns to cut neck opening. From neck opening, cut a 6″ opening down center of back.

Fold lining fabric in half, wrong side out, and pin. Pin linen piece to fabric. Trace outline of linen piece and neck and back openings. Remove linen and, keeping lining fabric pinned, cut along all lines. (When seamed, this will leave about ½″ overhang of linen on outside edges. Depending on the border trim of your linen, you may want more overhang. Trim fabric accordingly.)

Leaving right sides of 2 lining pieces facing and using a ¼″ seam allowance, sew outline only. (Leave neck and back opening unsewn.) Clip seam at curves. Turn lining right side out and press. (Now you have a double lining.)

Lay linen piece right side down on lining, and pin neck and back openings of linen to side of lining it faces (not both layers of lining). (See Figure.) Using ¼″ seam allowance, sew these two layers together. Bring linen through neck opening of lining so that linen is right side out. Remaining raw edge of lining will be middle of 3 layers. Turn raw edge of middle layer under ¼″ and slipstitch. Sew hook and eye at top of back opening.

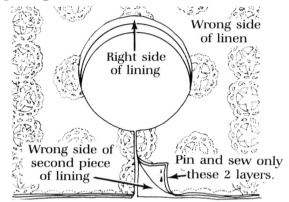

Right side of lining

Wrong side of linen

Wrong side of second piece of lining

Pin and sew only these 2 layers.

UNLINED COLLAR

MATERIALS:

    pattern on page 148
    oval or circular linen doily
    thread to match
    strip of elastic buttonhole loops
       (length of doily's radius)
    coordinating buttons

From pattern given, make a pattern for front neckline and 1 for back neckline. Fold linen in half, wrong side out, and crease along fold. Use patterns to cut neck opening. Cut straight line down center of back from neck opening to edge of doily.

Roll and whip neckline hem (or make narrow hem). To hem back opening, turn under fabric ¼″ and stitch. Turn under another ¼″ and hem. To hem lace section of back opening, use a machine zigzag stitch, then pull thread slightly to blend stitches into lace.

Trim buttonhole strip to exact length of back opening, and stitch to wrong side of left side. Sew buttons on right side opposite loops.

Needlepoint Treasures: Square by Square

In these needlepoint decorations, a blue-and-white checked tablecloth beneath bears and holly, ducks and wreaths, gives Christmas colors a whole new twist. And behind each creature, yellow and green wallpaper continues the colorful patterning.

Needlepoint the squares individually for tree ornaments, or, for the stocking, put squares together in latticework dotted by poinsettias. Worked with lustrous pearl cotton in a variety of stitches, deft hands can make showpieces of these decorations.

STOCKING

MATERIALS:
 patterns and charts on page 152
 pearl cotton and embroidery floss
  (for details, see chart)
 rotating tapestry or stretcher frame
  (optional)
 14-mesh mono interlocked canvas
  (14″ x 22″)
 14″ x 22″ green velvet
 1⅓ yards cording or 1⅓ yards cable
  cord and extra ⅛ yard velvet
 ½ yard white lining fabric
 thread to match

Transfer stocking outline to canvas and work needlepoint motifs from chart. Block needlepoint and allow to dry thoroughly.

Cut out stocking plus ⅝″ seam allowance.

Use purchased cording or make your own. To make cording, cut 2″-wide bias strips from velvet, and with wrong sides facing, wrap around cable cord. Trim seam allowance to ⅝″. Align raw edges of cording with raw edge of stocking front, right sides facing, and stitch around all edges except top. For front facing, cut a 2″ x 8½″ strip of velvet. With right sides of strip and stocking facing, machine-stitch along top edge.

Cut stocking back from velvet, adding a ⅝″ seam allowance and extra height as indicated on pattern. With right sides facing, machine-stitch front and back of stocking around all sides except top, stitching along cord seam. Clip curves, trim seam, and turn.

Cut two pieces for stocking lining, place right sides together and stitch, leaving top open. Clip curves, trim seams, and press open. Place lining inside stocking and tack at top edge. Turn down velvet cuff in back to cover raw edge of lining. Whipstitch to close. Make loop from velvet and stitch to top.

ORNAMENTS

MATERIALS (for each ornament):
 patterns and charts on page 153
 pearl cotton and embroidery floss
  (for details, see chart)
 rotating tapestry or stretcher frame
  (optional)
 14-mesh mono interlocked canvas (6″
  x 7½″)
 5½″ x 6″ scrap of velvet fabric
 thread to match
 gold thread

Mark a 3¾″ square on canvas and work needlepoint motifs from chart. Block needlepoint and allow to dry thoroughly. Cut out square, leaving ⅝″ seam allowance. Cut a 5½″ x 6″ rectangle from velvet. With right sides facing, pin and machine-stitch around 3 sides, leaving one side open. Clip fabric at curves and trim seam. Turn and slip-stitch opening closed. To hang, sew gold thread through top corner and tie in a knot.

Ribbon Rays
Make a Heavenly Angel

Gleaming ribbon rays crisscross behind a pearly winged angel in this distinctive holiday wall hanging. The earth tones used here harmonize with the lustrous brass and wood furnishings, but you can adapt to other color schemes. Canvas backing gives the moiré extra body, and stacked ribbon adds dimension to the angel's robe.

MATERIALS:
> **pattern on page 150**
> **⅝ yard beige moiré taffeta**
> **½ yard canvas**
> **approximately 14 yards ribbon**
>   **(assorted complementary colors,**
>   **patterns and widths)**
> **nylon "invisible" thread**
> **decorative thread**
> **22″ metal curtain rod**

Cut a 20″ x 26″ piece of taffeta and an 18″ x 24″ piece of canvas. With wrong sides facing, center canvas on taffeta and baste together. Baste together loosely in a grid pattern to hold layers together.

Transfer angel pattern to taffeta so that it's centered horizontally, and 6″ from the bottom and 7″ from the top.

Choose ribbon in coordinating colors and patterns of gold, pearl white, maroon, brown, and ecru. Layer narrow ribbon on wider ribbon for depth and use patterned ribbon for accents. Use photographs as a guide.

Following the numbered sequence on pattern, cut lengths of ribbon, 1 section at a time, and pin in place. Where other ribbon will cover ends, leave raw. Where a finished edge is needed, turn under edge of ribbon before stitching. Stitch with invisible thread or decorative thread as desired. When angel is finished, remove basting from taffeta. Fold taffeta to back of canvas and hem.

Use straightedge to sketch background rays. Cut ribbon for rays and stitch in place. Finish front edges of taffeta with ribbon, folding diagonally at corners as shown in photograph. Turn exposed corners of taffeta back and stitch.

Cut five 4½″ lengths of ribbon (same ribbon as used in edging), loop, and stitch ends to top back of hanging. Slip curtain rod through loops to hang.

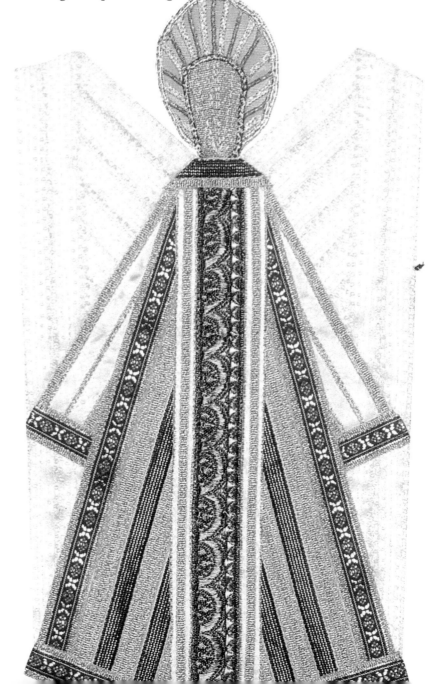

Reflections of Home

A homey glow radiates from these copper houses, evoking images of Christmases long ago. By adding a name or date, you can give a handmade gift that represents friendship year after year.

Metal tooling is the process of punching and indenting a sheet of soft metal, resulting in sculptured relief. A revival of an early American folk craft, this technique can be quickly learned by beginners and adjusted to numerous decorating possibilities.

When seeking additional patterns, choose designs with simple lines and little detail. To work from a photograph or drawing, trace the design's outline onto plain paper.

MATERIALS:
   patterns on page 137
   tracing paper
   fine-point black pen
   13½" x 6¼" copper tooling foil (36
      gauge)
   masking tape
   stack of newspapers (½" thick)
   ruler or T-square
   empty ballpoint pen
   copper-punching tool or icepick
   scissors
   liquid liver of sulfur (available at craft
      stores)
   small disposable paint brush
   clear spray sealer
   ⅛" satin ribbons for hanging

Transfer patterns to tracing paper with fine-point black pen. Cut a piece of tooling foil

slightly larger than pattern. Tape foil securely to newspapers. Tape traced pattern on top of foil.

Using a ruler as a guide, trace all lines on pattern with an empty ballpoint pen, pressing hard enough to indent foil through the pattern. If desired, personalize the ornament with a name or date on the bottom open area by writing with the empty pen. Check to be certain that all lines have been traced, and remove pattern, leaving the indented foil taped to newspapers.

With the punching tool, punch holes through the foil along indented lines, leaving as little space between holes as possible (see photograph). When punching is completed, remove foil, turn wrong side up, and tape to newspaper.

Again using a ruler and empty ballpoint pen, draw straight lines outside or inside rows of holes to give added dimension. Cut around the outside edge of the punched outline of the house. Punch a hole in top center of ornament, through which to run a ribbon loop for hanging.

To antique the ornaments, mix ½ teaspoon of liver of sulfur and ½ cup of water in a disposable container. (*Note:* Liver of sulfur is poisonous and should be kept out of reach of children.) Brush this solution onto the front of the ornament. It will immediately turn black. Rub the surface of the ornament with steel wool, to remove the black, until you get the desired antique effect. Rinse the ornament in cool water and dry it thoroughly.

Coat ornaments with a clear protective spray to prevent further discoloration. Hang ornament from a satin ribbon and use as a tree decoration or package tie.

A Rag Doll with Country Style

Come Christmas morning, little girls will squeeze this huggable, soft rag doll in delight. And for years to come, the doll's romantically fashioned dress and wide-eyed, rosy-cheeked expression will set her apart as a collectible in the popular country style.

MATERIALS:
   patterns on page 138
   1 yard (45"-wide) unbleached muslin (for body, bloomers, slip, and apron)
   scraps of brown felt or Ultrasuede (for shoes)
   ⅔ yd. (45"-wide) fabric (for dress)
   matching thread
   polyester stuffing
   small amount of acrylic paint (for face)
   natural twine (for hair)
   1 yd. lace (for slip bottom)
   small basket (optional)
   5" straw doll's hat
   embroidery floss or thin twine (for gathering shoes)
   craft glue
   two 7" pieces of ¼" elastic (for bloomers and slip)

Cut out patterns. Sew body pieces together around arms and head, leaving open at the bottom. Clip curves and turn right side out. Firmly stuff head and shoulders. Lightly stuff arms and hands. Sew legs, leaving tops open for stuffing. Clip curves and turn right side out. Firmly stuff feet and lightly stuff legs. To attach, turn bottom edge of body to inside ½". Insert raw edges of legs and pin. Zigzag-stitch together.

Lightly pencil doll's face, and paint. For hair, cut twine to desired lengths and unravel. Cover back and sides of head with water-diluted glue. Apply twine and cut to desired style. (Hat covers top of head.)

Sew bloomers' center seam from waist to large dots. Fold over waist ½" and sew to form casing, leaving an opening. Insert elastic, join ends, and stitch closed. Sew leg seams and hem. Turn right side out.

For slip, fold bottom edge under ½" and sew lace to underside. Sew center back seam. Fold waist over ½" and sew to form casing, leaving an opening. Insert elastic, then stitch closed.

For each shoe, fold top piece in half, right sides facing, and stitch back seam. With right sides facing, pin top to bottom of shoe and stitch. Turn right side out and slip shoes on doll's feet. Gather center of shoe top to fit doll's foot.

With right sides facing, sew dress bodice and neck facing pieces together at shoulders. Fold neck ruffle in half lengthwise, with wrong sides facing, and gather. With raw edges together, adjust ruffle gathers around bodice neck, stopping ¼" before each edge of center back. Pin facing over ruffle, right sides and raw edges together, and sew all layers together. Turn and press facing toward bodice, ruffle up. Topstitch around neck edge.

Gather upper sleeve as shown on pattern. With right sides facing, adjust gathers to fit sleeve opening in bodice; pin, and sew. Sew sleeve seams. Hem bottom of skirt and gather top skirt edge. With right sides facing, even gathers around waist of bodice and sew. Sew back seam from skirt bottom to waist. Dress doll and stitch dress opening closed. Turn under sleeves.

Sew both sets of apron bodice fronts and backs together at shoulder seams. With right sides facing, sew neck, arm, and side seams. Leave waist open for turning. Clip curves, turn, and press. Hem apron skirt and stitch side seams. Gather at the top. With right sides facing, sew skirt to bodice layer. Press seam allowance toward bodice, fold raw edge of facing under, and slip-stitch to skirt back. Put apron over dress and stitch back seam of bodice closed, leaving skirt portion open. Add hat and basket.

Festive Folk Dolls

Jolly cross-stitch peasant dolls can add a touch of folklore to holiday arrangements, or delight a little girl when she discovers them in her stocking. Red kerchiefs seem to wrap snugly under chins, and bright green apron pockets are perfect for holding little surprises. And all three dolls are worked from one chart—you just vary the thread count of the Aida cloth.

MATERIALS:
 charts on page 146
 9″ x 15″ 8-count Aida cloth (for large doll)
 8″ x 12″ 11-count Aida cloth (for medium doll)
 7″ x 12″ 14-count Aida cloth (for small doll)
 embroidery floss (for colors, see chart)
 9″ x 15″ woven iron-on interfacing (for large doll)
 white thread
 fiberfill
 scraps of white cotton fabric
 cardboard
 scraps of white felt

Follow chart to cross-stitch front, back, and apron of dolls, leaving ¼″ seam allowance around the finished work. Cut out. (For the large doll, back the Aida cloth with iron-on interfacing.)

With right sides facing, stitch front and back together, leaving bottom open. Turn right side out and stuff. Cut white fabric the same size as apron. With right sides facing, stitch together, leaving bottom open. Turn, press bottom raw edges to inside, and slip-stitch bottom and sides of apron to doll, following photograph.

Cut cardboard and felt to fit the bottom of doll. Slip cardboard inside bottom of doll, folding raw edges of Aida cloth over it. Cover bottom with felt and slip-stitch in place.

Pom-Poms Make These Sweaters Fun

Perk up a winter sweater with a pom-pom design. Sew brightly colored pom-poms to purchased sweaters for an irresistible combination.

MATERIALS:
  ready-made sweater
  ¼″ and ½″ pom-poms (green, red, black, and white)
  thread to match pom-poms

For the Christmas tree sweater, you will need 27 green ½" pom-poms, 8 black ¼" pom-poms, and 1 white ¼" pom-pom. Refer to photo for pom-pom placement. Larger tree is centered on back, 2 smaller trees go on each side of sweater front. Hand-stitch pom-poms to sweater, making several passes with the needle to secure. Sweaters should be hand-washed.

For the snowman sweater, you will need to get 36 white ½" pom-poms and 8 black ¼" pom-poms. Refer to photo for pom-pom placement. Snowman is centered on back of sweater. Remaining pom-poms should be randomly sewn to back and front of sweater to give the appearance of snowflakes.

Shadow Appliqué: Subtle Christmas Color

Shadowy holly leaves and berries, framed by lace, subtly dress up the apron and place mats shown here. Red and green cutouts slipped under voile are outline-stitched in place. On the apron, eyelet finishes the skirt, and lace with a red ribbon insert tops the bib and forms the neck strap. The set makes a lovely gift—but you may decide you want it for your holiday entertaining, instead!

PLACE MATS

MATERIALS:
   pattern on page 147
   ¾ yard (45″-wide) white broadcloth
   ¾ yard (45″-wide) white voile
   thread to match
   9 yards (½″) lace
   ½ yard lightweight fusible interfacing
   ⅛ yard red broadcloth
   ¼ yard green broadcloth
   fabric glue
   red and green embroidery floss

Prewash and iron all fabrics. Cut four 13″ x 19″ rectangles out of the white broadcloth and 4 of the same size out of the voile. With right sides of broadcloth and voile rectangles facing, stitch a ½″ seam around mat, leaving a 7″ opening in the center of 1 short side. Trim seams to ¼″, turn and press. The voile side is the top of the place mat.

Cut three 13″ and two 19″ pieces of lace for each place mat. Tack ends under ½″. Stitch lace 1½″ from edges on all but side with opening. On open side, stitch lace 4″ from edge.

Fuse interfacing to red and green fabric. For each place mat, cut out 8 green leaves and 2 red berries. Dab glue to interfacing side, slip between 2 layers of fabric and pat in place as shown on pattern. Pin or baste layers together to keep voile from slipping. Using 2 strands of embroidery floss, stitch through all layers to outline leaves in green and berries in red. Blind-stitch the side opening and sew lace flush on that edge.

APRON

MATERIALS:
    pattern on page 147
    1 yard (45"-wide) white broadcloth
    ½ yard (45"-wide) white voile
    thread to match
    2½ yards (½") lace
    ⅛ yard green broadcloth
    ⅛ yard red broadcloth
    ¼ yard lightweight fusible interfacing
    fabric glue
    red and green embroidery floss
    2 yards (4") flat eyelet lace
    1 yard lace with ribbon insert

Prewash and iron all fabrics. From white broadcloth, cut 20" x 45" skirt, 11" square bib, two 4" x 33" ties, and two 2½" x 17" waistbands. From voile, cut 11" square bib and 4½" x 45" border. Seam allowance is ½".

With right sides facing, sew voile and broadcloth bib pieces together on three sides. Trim seams to ⅛", turn, and press. Unsewn side is bottom of bib. Cut four 11" pieces of lace. On 2 pieces, tack ends under ½". Leave ends of 2 pieces unfinished. Sew a finished strip of lace 1½" from top edge of bib. Sew 2 unfinished pieces of lace 1" from side edges of bib.

Fuse interfacing to red and green fabric. Transfer and cut out 52 green leaves and 16 red berries. Dab glue on interfacing side of leaves and berries for bib. Following pattern for placement, slip leaves and berries between voile and broadcloth and push into place about ⅛" from top rows of lace. Pin or baste layers together to keep voile from slipping. With a double strand of floss, stitch through all layers to outline leaves in green and berries in red. To frame design, stitch remaining finished piece of lace across bib below design. (See photo detail.)

Pin voile border along bottom edge of skirt. Stitch 45" strip of lace along upper edge, to cover raw edge of voile. Following border pattern, begin in border center and glue groupings of leaves and berries about ⅜" apart. Secure and outline-stitch.

Gather eyelet lace for ruffle, and with right sides facing, stitch to lower edge of skirt. Hem side edges and ties.

Press under ½" on ends of waistband pieces. Gather skirt top onto one waistband, and, with right sides facing, stitch.

With right sides facing, pin waistband pieces, centered, on either side of bib bottom. Stitch the length of waistband. Press remaining waistband edge toward skirt and slip-stitch, covering stitching line.

Turn under unfinished ends of waistband, insert ties about 1", and stitch. For neck strap, tack lace with ribbon insert to one side of bib top, and adjust to proper length. Pin in place. Pin lace with ribbon along top edge of bib, turn ends under, and stitch through all layers.

A Basket for the Hearth

Ruffles and bows, made by dampening and then molding specially treated fabric, dress up an ordinary basket. It's ideal for holding kindling or goodies to give friends. For a personal touch, paint your own design after the fabric hardens.

MATERIALS:
   fruit basket (approx. 12″ x 21″)
   spray paint (optional)
   1 yard (40″-wide) Dip 'n Drape fabric
   2 yards ribbon (optional)
   gesso
   acrylic paints
   small brush
   clear gloss spray varnish

Finish basket with paint or sealer. To make ruffle and bows, cut 2 strips each from Dip 'n Drape fabric as follows: 5″ x 40″ ruffle, 5″ x 16″ bow ends, 5″ x 12″ bow. Fold all strips in half lengthwise.

To prepare fabric for application, dip strip in water and quickly pull between fingers to squeeze out excess water. (Fabric takes about 30 seconds to become pliable.)

Beginning at base of either handle, attach ¼″ of cut edge to inside of basket edge, and allow remainder of fabric to drape over outside edge. Proceed around entire edge of basket, pinching fabric to create ruffles on front of basket.

Wrap bow end around base of handle and cross in front. Fold both ends of bow strip to center, crimp, and place on crossed area of bow ends. Cover center with a small piece of fabric. Let harden overnight. To conceal cut edge of fabric, glue a strip of ribbon over edge inside basket.

When dry, paint fabric with gesso. With acrylic paint, decorate ruffle and bows. After paint dries, spray three coats of clear gloss varnish on basket, and let dry.

A Cozy, Ribbon-Laced Afghan

Snuggle under this thick, cozy afghan and get a whole new perspective on cold winter nights. Bright red-and-green ribbon lacing through rows of triple crochet makes the afghan as decorative as it is practical. When 'tis no longer the season, replace the Christmas colors with ribbon that accents a bedroom or den, and enjoy cuddly warmth as long as the weather permits. This afghan is sure to warm hearts as well as toes.

MATERIALS:
- **12 skeins (100 gr. or 3.5 oz.) 4-ply worsted weight acrylic yarn, off-white**
- **size K (10½") crochet hook (or size required to obtain gauge)**
- **13½ yards (¾"-wide) plaid ribbon**

GAUGE: 3 sts = 1", 5 rows = 2"

Ch 137. *Row 1*: 1 sc in 3rd ch from hook, * 1 dc in next ch, 1 sc in next ch *, repeat across row, ending with 1 dc in last ch, ch 2 (counts as first dc of next row), turn.

Row 2: Working through both loops, sk first dc, * 1 dc in sc of previous row, 1 sc in dc of previous row *, repeat across row, ending with 1 dc in ch 2 of previous row, ch 2, turn.

Repeat Row 2 for 6". On last row, ch 3, turn.

INSERTION: *Row A:* Sk first dc, tr in next sc and in each stitch across, ending with tr in ch 2 of previous row; 135 tr; ch 2, turn. *Row B:* Sk 1st tr, * 1 dc in next tr, 1 sc in next tr *, repeat across row ending with 1 dc in ch 3 of previous row, ch 2, turn. Repeat Row 2 three times. On last row, ch 3, turn.

Repeat Insertion 3 times and continue repeating Row 2 until total work measures 54". Ch 3, turn.

Repeat Insertion pattern until there are 4 tr rows. Repeat Row 2 for 6" beyond last tr. Tie off.

FRINGE: Cut strands of yarn 9" long. Knot 6 strands in each dc across ends of afghan. Trim yarn ends. Steam lightly if necessary.

RIBBON TRIM: Cut 8 pieces of ribbon 60" long. In each row of insertion, leave about a 5" tail and weave ribbon over 2 tr and under 2 tr to end of row. Fold excess ribbon on each end to back of afghan and weave under several tr to secure.

Standard Crochet Abbreviations

st(s)—stitch(es)
ch—chain
sk—skip
sc—single crochet
dc—double crochet
tr—triple crochet
* * Instructions between asterisks should be worked according to instructions that follow the asterisks.

Nightshirt Santa

Sure to delight the child in everyone is this quaint wooden replica of St. Nick making ready for a long winter's nap. The arrival of this novel portrayal of Santa may well become one of those happily anticipated heralds of the day.

MATERIALS:
 patterns on page 144
 16″ (1 x 6) pine
 ¼″ plywood (scrap)
 jigsaw or band saw
 sandpaper
 acrylic paints
 wood stain
 white glue
 ⅜ yard (45″-wide) red fabric
 matching thread
 beige pom-pom
 two ½″ brads
 tiny purchased glasses or brass wire
  bent to form glasses
 polyester stuffing or fleece (for beard
  and hair)

Transfer pattern for Santa to 1 x 6, and pattern for arms to plywood. From 1 x 6, cut a 2¼″ x 6″ piece, and bevel top edges for a base. Sand all surfaces. Paint body and arms flesh-colored. Transfer shoes and facial details. Paint following photo. Stain base and glue Santa in center.

Transfer pattern for Santa's cap to fabric and cut out. With right sides facing, sew side seam and turn. Sew pom-pom on tip. Paint holly motif as shown in photograph, leaving enough room to turn cap edge under.

Cut out nightshirt pattern from fabric. With right sides facing, sew from small dots at neckline to sleeve opening, and from sleeve opening to large dots on side seams. Hem the bottom, keeping corners round. Turn sleeve edges under ½″ and hem.

Nail left arm to body side, leaving loose enough to move, and adjust position. Dress Santa in nightshirt. Turn neck edge under. Slip right arm through bottom of sleeve. Nail into place from the front through shirt until brad is almost flush. Slip brad through fabric and hammer rest of the way in. Glue glasses at the sides of the head and let dry. Glue hair and beard into place. Fold under bottom of nightcap and glue cap to head, tucking hair underneath.

Quick! Make Gifts to Have on Hand

Decorated containers, painted carafes, burlap bags. . . . The gifts you see here go together so quickly you could fill Santa's bag. Make a big batch before the holiday rush, and you'll be ready when it's time to exchange gifts.

Enchant friends and family with tiny, whimsical scenes atop jars of goodies. Toys, ornaments, beads, and baubles offer a wealth of material. Start combining wee flora and fauna, and watch a diminutive world unfold.

Here you see some of the possibilities. Tiny teddies sit on mounds of presents in a forest of little trees. Mice peep around a present, and baby bunnies perch between little cones. Craft glue holds the decorations

in place, and odds and ends of ribbon tie it all together.

For friends who enjoy the fruit of the vine, extend a wish for happy holly days with a moose carafe. Its clever design is so quick to paint, you can make several for gifts and keep one on hand for holiday entertaining.

And whether you're looking for unusual gift wrapping, or want to decorate a corner of your home, bright and festive burlap bags could be the answer. Place a brick inside one, and you have a novel bookend. Slip a friend's favorite wine inside, and you have clever and reusable gift wrap.

These bags are as easy to assemble as they are versatile. Instructions for the carafe and burlap bags follow.

BURLAP BAG WRAP

MATERIALS (for 1 bag):
½ yard (36″-wide) burlap
thread to match
1 brick
bows and ornaments (as desired)

Cut a 16″ x 18″ piece of burlap and fold in half for a 16″ x 9″ rectangle. With a ½″ seam allowance, sew 1 short side and remaining long side. Turn right side out. Make a 3″ fringe at open end (top) by pulling out horizontal threads. (Keep pulled threads together to use as a tie for the bag.)

To make pocket, cut a 7″ x 13″ piece of burlap and fold in half for a 7″ x 6½″ rectangle. Folded side will be top of pocket. With a ½″ seam allowance, sew the two sides and turn right side out. Turn remaining edges to inside and slip-stitch closed. Sew pocket on bag so that it's centered horizontally and 1″ from bottom.

Place brick inside bag, use pulled threads to cinch bag over brick, and decorate as desired.

HOLLY DAYS WINE CARAFE

MATERIALS:
pattern on page 147
½ liter wine carafe
gloss enamel paints for models
(colors indicated on pattern)
20″ (⅞″-wide) craft ribbon
thin-tipped, water-base marker
thin ribbon and gift tag (optional)

Use marker to transfer pattern to side of carafe opposite raised medallion. Paint large areas first, then details. Use white paint for bow details and polka dots, and paint message last, following photograph.

Tie ribbon in a bow around neck of carafe. If desired, tie a gift tag to the bow with ribbon.

Note: Hand-wash carafe only. Do not place in dishwasher.

Say Welcome with Cross-Stitch

When out-of-town company or family visit for the holidays, it's the small, unexpected touches that they will appreciate and remember. This year, welcome your visitors with cross-stitched guest towels.

Greetings are stitched onto a special even-weave ribbon, which is attached to the towel with a fusible fabric strip. Personalize the message to fit the guest and the holiday. This could make a thoughtful gift or a cordial reception for an annual visitor. And it's an imaginative and hospitable way to display your handiwork.

MATERIALS:
   charts on page 146
   guest towels (Christmas colors)
   Ribband (decorative ribbon with
      woven arca for cross-stitching)
   rcd, green, and gold metallic
      embroidery floss
   ¾"-wide Stitch Witchery (2-sided
      fusible fabric)

Cut ribbon in strips 1½" longer than front of towels. Using designs from charts, cross-stitch names, holiday motifs, and seasonal messages. Cut fusible fabric strip the same length as ribbon. Position ribbon over fusible fabric on towel and tuck ends to back. Using pressing cloth, iron to fuse both sides following manufacturer's directions.

Celebrations from the Kitchen

Coming inside on a cold December day, how wonderful it is to be engulfed by sweetness and warmth. A Christmas kitchen flavors the whole experience of the season. Hot chocolate toasts the inside and outside of the coldest little explorer. A homemade fruitcake shortens the distance between relatives in different towns, and hot, spicy punch turns tree trimming into party time.

Nourishment for body and soul—that's the purpose of food prepared during the holidays. Pause to remember your childhood Christmases—a special dessert you anticipated all year, milk and cookies put out for Santa, a big turkey dinner that left you sleepy and content. Through cooking, we express love for family members, honor visitors, and pamper children. For Southerners, it's a tradition and a source of pride. It's part and parcel of our reputation for hospitality.

When company comes to a Southern home, the table is usually spread with enough food to fill the guests twice over. When the visitors are family, like as not they'll leave with a package—be it half of a cake, an extra loaf of freshly baked bread, or part of a Christmas ham.

Whether you're interested in new twists for the traditional Christmas dinner or want refreshments for strolling carolers and tired shoppers, there's something for you in this chapter. Choose the recipes here that suit your style for Christmas; then mix, taste, bake, and enjoy.

Gather the Family for Holiday Dinner

From the first mouth-watering whiff that wafts from the kitchen to the hearty and handsome dishes that debut in the dining room, from the ring of the door bell to the circle of loved ones around your table, Christmas dinner is a celebration to nourish body and soul.

For this year's feast, try the menu offered here. Although the foods are mostly traditional, these recipes feature special stuffings, seasonings, and sauces to tantalize the taste buds.

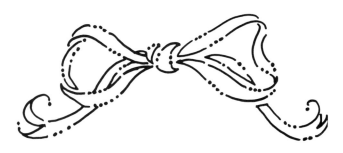

Fresh Mushroom Soup
Stuffed Turkey Breast
Oyster Casserole
Sweet Potatoes with Apples
Brussels Sprouts with Pecans
Candied Brandied Cranberries
Cheesy Bundt Bread
Toasted Almond Croquembouche
(Menu serves 12.)

Spreads like this one explain that old expression—the groaning board. Left to right: Stuffed Turkey Breast, Candied Brandied Cranberries, Oyster Casserole, Sweet Potatoes with Apples, Brussels Sprouts with Pecans, and Toasted Almond Croquembouche.

84

Christmas dinner is a time to bring out all the best: china, crystal, silver, candles, and of course, food. For a festive centerpiece, poinsettias, holly, and greenery form dramatic diagonals across the dining table.

FRESH MUSHROOM SOUP

1½ cups chopped green onions with
     tops
½ cup butter or margarine, melted
1 pound fresh mushrooms, sliced
¼ cup plus 2 tablespoons all-purpose
     flour
¼ teaspoon white pepper
3 cups chicken broth
3 cups milk

Sauté onion in butter in a Dutch oven 3 to 4 minutes or until tender. Add mushrooms, and sauté 2 minutes. Stir in flour and white pepper; cook over medium heat, stirring constantly, 2 minutes. Gradually add chicken broth and milk, stirring until smooth; bring mixture just to a boil over low heat, stirring constantly. Yield: 9 cups.

STUFFED TURKEY BREAST

1 (12-ounce) package bacon,
     chopped
1 cup chopped onion
3 (10-ounce) packages frozen
     chopped spinach, thawed and
     well drained
2 eggs
1 cup ricotta cheese
¾ teaspoon garlic salt
¾ teaspoon dried whole oregano
½ teaspoon freshly ground pepper
1 (9- to 10-pound) turkey breast,
     boned
⅓ cup butter or margarine, melted

Sauté bacon in a large skillet until crisp; transfer bacon to paper towels using a slotted spoon, and drain well. Pour off all but ¼ cup bacon drippings; add onion to drippings in skillet, and sauté until tender. Stir in spinach; cook, uncovered, over medium heat 5 minutes, stirring frequently. Cool slightly.

Combine eggs and cheese in a medium bowl; blend well. Stir in spinach mixture, spices, and bacon; mix well.

Lay turkey breast flat on waxed paper, skin side down. Remove tendons, and trim fat with a sharp knife, keeping skin intact. Starting from the center, slice horizontally (parallel with skin) through the thickest part of each side of breast almost to the outer edge; flip cut piece and breast fillets over to enlarge breast. Pound turkey breast to flatten it and form a more even thickness.

Spread spinach mixture in center of turkey breast, leaving a 2-inch border at sides. Fold in sides of turkey breast over filling. Roll up turkey breast over filling, pulling skin over exposed meat to seal roll (roll should be about 13 to 16 inches long); secure with skewers.

Tie roll together securely in several places with string; place roll, seam side down, on a rack in a roasting pan. Pour melted butter evenly over roll. Bake at 425° for 40 minutes. Reduce oven temperature to 350°, and bake an additional 55 minutes or until done. Let stand 15 minutes before slicing. Yield: 12 to 15 servings.

OYSTER CASSEROLE

      4 (12-ounce) containers oysters
      1 cup chopped green onions with
          tops
      1 cup minced fresh parsley
      2 cups cracker crumbs
      ¾ cup butter or margarine, melted
      3 tablespoons lemon juice
      1 teaspoon dry mustard
      1 tablespoon plus 2 teaspoons
          Worcestershire sauce
          Additional minced fresh parsley

Drain oysters; pat dry with paper towels. Arrange oysters in a 12- x 8- x 2-inch glass baking dish; top with layers of green onion, 1 cup parsley, and cracker crumbs. Combine next 4 ingredients, mixing well; pour evenly over cracker crumbs.

Bake at 350° for 30 to 35 minutes. Arrange minced parsley as a border around casserole. Yield: 12 servings.

SWEET POTATOES WITH APPLES

      6 large sweet potatoes (about 5
          pounds)
      3 tablespoons frozen orange juice
          concentrate, thawed and
          undiluted
      2 tablespoons water
      2 tablespoons honey
      1 tablespoon butter or margarine,
          melted
      ¼ cup sugar
      2 Golden Delicious apples, sliced
          ⅛-inch thick
     20 large marshmallows, halved

Cook sweet potatoes in boiling water 25 minutes or until tender. Let cool to the touch. Peel potatoes, and place in a large mixing bowl.

Combine orange juice concentrate, water, honey, and butter; mix well. Add sugar and ⅓ cup orange juice mixture to potatoes. Reserve remaining juice mixture. Beat potato mixture at medium speed of an electric mixer until smooth and fluffy. Spoon potato mixture into a greased, shallow 2½-quart casserole, spreading top smooth. Arrange apple slices over potatoes; brush apples with remaining orange juice concentrate mixture. Bake, uncovered, at 350° for 20 minutes. Arrange marshmallow halves over apples; continue baking an additional 20 minutes or until marshmallows are puffed and lightly browned. Yield: 12 servings.

BRUSSELS SPROUTS WITH PECANS

2 pounds fresh brussels sprouts or
    4 (10-ounce) packages frozen
    brussels sprouts
½ cup butter or margarine
1 cup coarsely chopped pecans
1 (2-ounce) jar diced pimiento,
    drained
¼ cup minced fresh parsley
2 tablespoons lemon juice

Trim and wash brussels sprouts. Cut a small cross in core of each with a sharp knife. Cover and cook in a small amount of boiling salted water for 5 to 8 minutes or until tender. (If using frozen brussels sprouts, cook according to package directions.) Drain and place in a serving dish; keep warm.

Melt butter in a skillet over medium heat; add pecans, and sauté until butter is golden and pecans are lightly toasted. Remove from heat; stir in remaining ingredients. Pour over brussels sprouts, and serve immediately. Yield: 12 servings.

CANDIED BRANDIED CRANBERRIES

3 (12-ounce) packages (about 9 cups)
    fresh cranberries
3 cups sugar
½ cup brandy

Arrange cranberries evenly in a single layer in 2 lightly greased jellyroll pans; pour sugar evenly over cranberries in each pan. Cover tightly with aluminum foil; bake at 350° for 1 hour. Spoon cranberries into a large serving bowl; add brandy, and mix well. Cool completely. Serve at room temperature, or refrigerate up to 1 week, and serve chilled. Yield: 12 servings.

CHEESY BUNDT BREAD

1 cup (4 ounces) shredded Cheddar
    cheese
¼ cup butter or margarine, softened
½ teaspoon Italian seasoning
¼ teaspoon garlic or onion powder
¼ cup sesame seeds
2½ cups all-purpose flour, divided
2 tablespoons sugar
1 teaspoon salt
2 packages dry yeast
½ cup milk
½ cup water
¼ cup butter or margarine
1 egg

Insert knife blade in food processor bowl. Combine first 4 ingredients in processor bowl; top with cover, and process until smooth, scraping bowl occasionally. Set aside.

Generously grease a 10-inch Bundt pan; sprinkle sesame seeds evenly in pan, coating well. Set aside.

Combine 1½ cups flour, sugar, salt, and yeast in a large mixing bowl; mix well. Combine milk, water, and butter in a small saucepan; cook over low heat until mixture reaches 120° on a thermometer, stirring constantly. (The butter does not need to melt completely.)

Add warm milk mixture and egg to flour mixture. Beat at low speed of an electric mixer until moistened; continue beating at medium speed 3 minutes. Gradually stir in remaining 1 cup flour to make a stiff batter.

Spoon half of batter evenly into prepared pan, spreading to cover bottom of pan. Spoon cheese filling evenly over batter; top with remaining batter, spreading to cover filling. Cover pan with plastic wrap; let rise in a warm place (85°), free from drafts, 1 hour or until batter rises to within ¾- to 1-inch from top of pan. Bake at 350° for 35 to 40 minutes or until loaf sounds hollow when tapped. Invert immediately onto a wire rack; cool completely before slicing. Yield: one 10-inch loaf.

TOASTED ALMOND CROQUEMBOUCHE

1½ cups water
¾ cup butter or margarine
1½ cups all-purpose flour
¼ teaspoon salt
6 eggs
   Amaretto Cream
   Almond Caramel Glaze

Combine water and butter in a large saucepan; bring to a boil. Combine flour and salt; add to butter mixture all at once, stirring vigorously over low heat until mixture leaves sides of pan and forms a smooth ball. Remove from heat, and cool slightly.

Add eggs, one at a time, beating with a wooden spoon after each addition; then beat until batter is smooth.

Drop batter by tablespoonfuls 2 inches apart onto lightly greased baking sheets, forming 32 cream puffs. Bake at 400° for 30 minutes or until golden brown. Cool on wire racks, away from drafts.

Slice off top one-third of cream puffs using a serrated knife. Fill bottoms with Amaretto Cream; replace tops. Stack cream puffs in a pyramid shape on a serving platter, beginning with a base of 16 cream puffs. Drizzle about ¾ cup Almond Caramel Glaze over pyramid. Serve with remaining Almond Caramel Glaze. Yield: 32 cream puffs.

Amaretto Cream:

   6 egg yolks, beaten
1⅔ cups milk, divided
   ⅔ cup sugar
   ⅔ cup all-purpose flour
   2 tablespoons butter or margarine, softened
   ⅓ cup amaretto
   1 teaspoon almond extract
   1 teaspoon vanilla extract

Combine egg yolks and ⅔ cup milk in a heavy saucepan; blend well using a wire whisk. Combine sugar and flour; add to yolk mixture, mixing until smooth. Then stir in remaining 1 cup milk. Cook over medium heat, stirring constantly, until mixture is very thick. Cool slightly; blend in butter, amaretto, and flavorings. Cover with plastic wrap, and chill thoroughly. Yield: about 2¾ cups.

Almond Caramel Glaze:

1½ cups sugar
   ¾ cup boiling water
   ¼ cup amaretto
   ½ cup slivered almonds, toasted

Place sugar in a heavy skillet or saucepan; cook over low heat, stirring constantly, until sugar melts and forms a light brown syrup. Gradually add boiling water in a very slow, steady stream, stirring constantly with a wire whisk. (Do not add water rapidly; mixture may bubble up and overflow, or may form lumps.) Simmer 5 minutes or until mixture reaches small-thread stage (220°) on a candy thermometer. Remove from heat, and stir in amaretto and almonds. Cool to room temperature. Yield: 1⅓ cups.

Note: Cream puffs may be prepared, filled, and refrigerated up to 1 day in advance. Assemble pyramid up to 2 hours before serving.

Christmas Morning Breakfast

Before adults and children alike scatter to try out new toys, tempt your family with the delicious aromas of broiling ham, pancakes on the griddle, and cinnamon-spiced hot chocolate. A scrumptious breakfast will start the day off right.

Orange-Spiced Ham
Hot Cranberry Compote
Honey-Poached Pears
Buttermilk Waffles with Orange Butter
Almond Tea or Orange Tea
South-of-the-Border Hot Chocolate
(Menu serves 10.)

ORANGE-SPICED HAM

> 2 (1-inch-thick) slices cooked ham
>   (about 1½ pounds each)
> 2 cups ginger ale
> 2 cups orange juice
> 1 cup firmly packed brown sugar
> ¼ cup plus 2 tablespoons vegetable
>   oil
> 2 tablespoons wine vinegar
> 1 tablespoon plus 1 teaspoon dry
>   mustard
> 1½ teaspoons ground ginger
> 1 teaspoon ground cloves
>   Fresh collard greens or spinach
>   (optional)

Score fat edges of ham, and place ham in a shallow baking pan. Combine next 8 ingredients; pour over ham slices. Cover and let stand at room temperature 1 hour or refrigerate overnight, spooning marinade over ham occasionally.

Broil ham 6 inches from heat source about 10 minutes on each side, brushing frequently with marinade. Heat remaining marinade, and serve with ham. Serve ham on a bed of collard greens, if desired. Yield: 10 to 12 servings.

HOT CRANBERRY COMPOTE

> 3 cups chopped apple
> 2 cups fresh cranberries
> 2 teaspoons lemon juice
> 1 cup sugar
> 1⅓ cups quick-cooking oats, uncooked
> 1 cup chopped walnuts
> ⅓ cup firmly packed light brown
>   sugar
> ½ cup butter or margarine, melted

Combine apples, cranberries, and lemon juice in a lightly greased, shallow 2-quart casserole; toss well. Pour sugar evenly over fruit.

Combine remaining ingredients, mixing well; sprinkle over sugar layer. Bake, uncovered, at 350° for 1 hour. Yield: 10 to 12 servings.

Waffles may get the kids' attention long enough to have breakfast. Front to back: Buttermilk Waffles, Orange Butter, South-of-the-Border Hot Chocolate, Orange-Spiced Ham, and Honey-Poached Pears. To make the ribbon angel hanging in the window, see page 62.

With more than a hint of honey, these poached pears are a subtle and different taste sensation—an alternative to standard citrus fruit. Serve Honey-Poached Pears in a shallow serving dish filled with whipped cream and garnish with strips of orange rind.

HONEY-POACHED PEARS

10 pears
   Lemon juice
 6 cups water
 2 cups honey
¼ cup lemon juice
 4 (3-inch) sticks cinnamon
   Whipping cream
   Orange rind strips (optional)

Peel pears, leaving stem intact. Trim bottom of each pear to form a flat base. Brush pears with small amount lemon juice as they are peeled, to prevent discoloration.

Combine next 4 ingredients in a large Dutch oven; bring to a boil. Add pears; cover, reduce heat, and simmer 15 to 25 minutes or until pears are tender.

Beat whipping cream just until thickened (but not stiff); pour into a shallow serving dish. Stand pears upright in cream; garnish with orange rind strips, if desired. Serve immediately. Yield: 10 servings.

BUTTERMILK WAFFLES

 5 cups sifted cake flour
 1 tablespoon plus 2 teaspoons
     baking powder
1¼ teaspoons baking soda
½ teaspoon salt
 5 eggs, separated
 3 cups plus 2 tablespoons buttermilk
1¼ cups vegetable oil
   Pecan halves (optional)
   Candied cherries (optional)
   Orange Butter
   Honey

Combine first 4 ingredients; stir well. Beat egg yolks; add yolks, buttermilk, and oil to dry ingredients, mixing well.

Beat egg whites (at room temperature) until soft peaks form; fold into batter. Pour about one-fifth of batter into a hot, lightly oiled waffle iron, spreading batter almost to edges. Cook about 5 minutes or until done. Repeat process with remaining batter. Garnish with pecans and cherries, if desired. Serve with Orange Butter and honey. Yield: 20 (4-inch) waffles.

Orange Butter:

    1 cup butter, softened
    2 tablespoons grated orange rind
    ¼ cup orange juice

Beat butter and rind until fluffy; gradually add orange juice, beating well. Store in refrigerator; serve at room temperature. Yield: 1¼ cups.

ALMOND TEA

    2½ cups water
    1 cup sugar
    4 to 6 regular tea bags
    ½ cup lemon juice
    2 quarts water
    1 teaspoon vanilla extract
    1 teaspoon almond extract

Combine 2½ cups water and sugar in a saucepan; bring to a boil, stirring until sugar melts. Add tea bags; remove from heat. Cover and let stand 5 minutes. Remove tea bags; stir in lemon juice. Cool; store tea concentrate in a jar in refrigerator for up to 1 week.

To serve, combine tea concentrate and 2 quarts water in a large saucepan; bring to a boil. Remove from heat, and stir in flavorings. Serve immediately. Yield: 11 cups.

ORANGE TEA

    6 regular-size tea bags
    2 quarts water
    3 tablespoons orange juice
        concentrate, undiluted
    ½ cup honey

Place tea bags and water in a large saucepan; bring to a boil. Cover, remove from heat, and let stand 5 minutes. Remove tea bags; stir in orange juice and honey. Serve hot. Yield: 8½ cups.

SOUTH-OF-THE-BORDER HOT CHOCOLATE

    ⅔ cup sugar
    2 teaspoons ground cinnamon
    1 cup milk
    4 (1-ounce) squares unsweetened
        chocolate
    7 cups milk
    1½ cups whipping cream (optional)
    ¼ cup sifted powdered sugar
        (optional)
        About 10 (4-inch) sticks cinnamon
        (optional)

Combine sugar and ground cinnamon in a large, heavy saucepan; stir in 1 cup milk. Add chocolate; cook over medium heat, stirring constantly, until chocolate melts. Stir in 7 cups milk; cook until thoroughly heated, stirring constantly with a wire whisk.

If whipped cream topping is desired, beat whipping cream until foamy; gradually add powdered sugar, beating until soft peaks form. Place cinnamon sticks in individual cups, if desired; fill cups with hot chocolate, and top each cup with a dollop of whipped cream. Yield: about 9 cups.

Breads

CHOCOLATE MACAROON MUFFINS

2 cups all-purpose flour
½ cup sugar
3 tablespoons cocoa
1 tablespoon baking powder
¼ teaspoon salt
1 egg, beaten
1 cup milk
⅓ cup vegetable oil
    Macaroon Filling

Combine first 5 ingredients in a large bowl; make a well in center of mixture. Combine egg, milk, and oil; add to dry ingredients, stirring just until moistened. Spoon into greased muffin pans, filling one-third full. Spoon 2 teaspoons Macaroon Filling in center of each muffin cup; spoon remaining batter over top, filling each muffin cup two-thirds full. Bake at 400° for 20 minutes. Serve warm. Yield: 1 dozen.

Macaroon Filling:

1 cup flaked coconut
¼ cup sweetened condensed milk
¼ teaspoon almond extract

Combine all ingredients, mixing well. Yield: ½ cup.

NUTTY DANISH PASTRY

½ cup butter or margarine
1 cup all-purpose flour
2 tablespoons water
½ cup butter or margarine
1 cup water
1 cup all-purpose flour
3 eggs
1 teaspoon vanilla extract
    Caramel Frosting
½ cup chopped pecans, divided

Cut ½ cup butter (at refrigerator temperature) into 1 cup flour with a pastry blender until mixture resembles coarse meal. Sprinkle 2 tablespoons water evenly over surface; stir with a fork until all dry ingredients are moistened. Shape mixture into 2 equal balls. Roll out each ball on an ungreased baking sheet, and trim to make each a 12- x 3-inch rectangle.

Combine ½ cup butter and 1 cup water in a saucepan; bring to a boil. Add 1 cup flour, all at once; reduce heat to low, and cook, stirring vigorously, until mixture forms a ball and leaves sides of pan. Remove from heat; cool 5 minutes.

Add eggs, one at a time, beating well after each addition. Beat in vanilla. Spoon mixture evenly over each pastry rectangle, spreading to edges. Bake pastries at 350° for 55 minutes.

Spread each pastry with Caramel Frosting while warm, and sprinkle each with ¼ cup chopped pecans. Serve pastries warm or at room temperature. Yield: two 12- x 3-inch pastries.

Caramel Frosting:

¼ cup butter or margarine
½ cup firmly packed brown sugar
1½ to 2 tablespoons milk
1½ cups sifted powdered sugar
½ teaspoon vanilla extract

Melt butter in a small saucepan. Add brown sugar, and cook 1 minute over low heat. Stir in remaining ingredients; beat with an electric mixer until smooth, adding more milk if necessary to make frosting a good spreading consistency. Yield: about 1½ cups.

Introduce these quick bread recipes into your holiday baking repertoire. Clockwise from back: Pigs' Ears, Nutty Danish Pastry, Fresh Lemon Muffins, and Chocolate Macaroon Muffins.

FRESH LEMON MUFFINS

½ cup butter or margarine
½ cup sugar
2 eggs
1 tablespoon grated lemon rind
3 tablespoons lemon juice
1 cup all-purpose flour
1 teaspoon baking powder
⅛ teaspoon salt
2 tablespoons sugar
¼ teaspoon ground cinnamon

Cream butter; gradually add ½ cup sugar, beating until light and fluffy. Add eggs, one at a time, beating well after each addition. Stir in lemon rind and juice. Combine flour, baking powder, and salt; add to creamed mixture, mixing well.

Spoon batter into greased miniature (1¾-inch) muffin pans, filling two-thirds full. Combine 2 tablespoons sugar and cinnamon; sprinkle evenly over each muffin. Bake at 375° for 15 minutes. Yield: about 2½ dozen.

OATMEAL SCONES

⅓ cup raisins
⅓ cup boiling water
1¼ cups all-purpose flour
¼ cup sugar
1 teaspoon baking powder
½ teaspoon baking soda
¼ teaspoon salt
¼ cup butter or margarine
¼ cup shortening
1 cup regular oats, uncooked
⅓ cup buttermilk
Melted butter

Combine raisins and boiling water; let stand 1 hour.

Combine flour, sugar, baking powder, soda, and salt in a medium mixing bowl; cut in butter and shortening with pastry blender until mixture resembles coarse meal. Drain raisins; add raisins and oats to flour mixture. Stir in buttermilk, mixing just until dry ingredients are moistened.

Turn dough out onto a floured surface, and knead 6 to 8 times. Roll dough into a 7-inch circle, and cut into 8 equal wedges. Place wedges on an ungreased baking sheet; brush with melted butter. Bake at 375° for 15 minutes. Serve warm. Yield: 8 scones.

ALMOND KRINGLE

2 packages dry yeast
1 teaspoon sugar
½ cup warm water (105° to 115°)
½ cup milk
½ cup sugar
½ cup butter or margarine
1 teaspoon salt
2 eggs, beaten
5½ cups all-purpose flour, divided
Almond Filling
1 egg white
1 teaspoon water
3 tablespoons sliced almonds

Dissolve yeast and 1 teaspoon sugar in warm water in a large bowl.

Combine milk, ½ cup sugar, butter, and salt in a saucepan; cook over medium heat, stirring constantly, until butter melts. Remove from heat, and cool to 105° to 115°. Add to yeast mixture. Stir in eggs and 2 cups flour; mix well. Gradually stir in remaining flour.

Turn dough out onto a floured surface, and knead until smooth and elastic (about 8 to 10 minutes). Place dough in a well-greased bowl, turning to grease top. Cover and let rise in a warm place (85°), free from drafts, 1½ hours or until doubled in bulk.

Punch dough down, and divide into thirds. Roll out each third into a 30- x 4-inch rectangle on a floured surface. Spread each with ½ cup Almond Filling. Roll up each rectangle jellyroll fashion, beginning at long end; pinch seams and ends to seal. Twist into pretzel shapes, and place on ungreased baking sheets.

Combine egg white and water; brush on bread shapes. Sprinkle each with 1 tablespoon almonds. Let rise in a warm place (85°), free from drafts, 1 hour or until doubled in bulk. Bake at 350° for 25 to 30 minutes; cover loosely with aluminum foil during last 10 minutes to prevent excess browning, if necessary. Yield: 3 loaves.

Almond Filling:

  1 (8-ounce) can almond paste
  ½ cup butter or margarine, softened
  ½ cup sugar
  ½ cup chopped candied citron

Combine all ingredients, mixing well. Yield: 1½ cups.

CARAMEL PECAN COFFEECAKE

  2 cups all-purpose flour
  ¾ cup sugar
  2½ teaspoons baking powder
  ¼ teaspoon salt
  ½ cup shortening
  1 tablespoon instant coffee granules
  2 eggs, beaten
  ⅔ cup milk
    Pecan Filling

Combine first 4 ingredients in a medium mixing bowl; make a well in center of mixture. Melt shortening; add coffee granules, stirring until dissolved. Combine eggs, milk, and shortening mixture; add to dry ingredients, stirring just until moistened.

Pour batter into a greased 9-inch square baking pan. Spread Pecan Filling over top; cut through filling and batter with a knife to marble. Bake at 375° for 25 to 30 minutes. Yield: one 9-inch coffeecake.

Pecan Filling:

  2 tablespoons butter or margarine
  ¾ cup firmly packed brown sugar
  1 egg, beaten
  ⅓ cup milk
  ⅓ cup chopped pecans

Combine first 4 ingredients in a small saucepan; cook over medium heat 4 minutes, stirring constantly. Remove from heat, and stir in pecans. Yield: about 1 cup.

CHOCOLATE APPLESAUCE BREAD

  1½ cups all-purpose flour
  1¼ cups sugar
  1 teaspoon baking soda
  ¼ teaspoon baking powder
  ¼ teaspoon salt
  ½ teaspoon ground cinnamon
  ¼ teaspoon ground nutmeg
  ⅓ cup butter or margarine
  2 (1-ounce) squares unsweetened
    chocolate
  ½ cup unsweetened applesauce
  2 eggs, beaten
  ½ cup chopped walnuts

Combine first 7 ingredients in a large bowl, mixing well; set aside.

Melt butter and chocolate in a heavy saucepan over low heat. Add chocolate mixture, applesauce, eggs, and walnuts to flour mixture, and mix well.

Pour batter into a greased and floured 9- x 5- x 3-inch loafpan. Bake at 350° for 50 to 55 minutes or until a wooden pick inserted in center comes out clean. Cool bread in pan 10 minutes; remove from pan, and cool completely on a wire rack. Yield: 1 loaf.

With a twist of a fork while cooking, you can turn pastry circles into Pigs' Ears. These unusual shapes are dipped in syrup and chopped pecans after cooking.

PIGS' EARS

  1 **cup all-purpose flour**
  ½ **teaspoon baking powder**
  ¼ **teaspoon salt**
  1 **egg**
  3 **tablespoons water**
    Vegetable oil
    About 1½ cups cane syrup
    Finely chopped pecans

Combine flour, baking powder, and salt in a small mixing bowl. Combine egg and water; add to flour mixture, and mix well. Divide dough into 12 equal parts, and roll each into a ball. Roll out balls of dough very thin on a lightly floured surface; stack rolled dough

between pieces of waxed paper to prevent drying.

Pour about 2 inches oil into a heavy saucepan; heat to 375°. Drop a pastry circle into hot oil; using a long-handled fork, immediately stick the tines in the center of the pastry, and twist quickly. Hold until set (the far side of the pastry will fold over on itself, forming an "ear"); cook until golden brown on both sides, and drain well on paper towels. Repeat procedure with remaining pastry.

Pour syrup into a heavy saucepan, and bring to a boil. Cook 5 to 10 minutes, stirring occasionally. Dip each "ear" in hot syrup, coating well on both sides. Sprinkle with chopped pecans. Let cool slightly on buttered waxed paper. Serve warm or at room temperature. Yield: 1 dozen.

APRICOT STREUSEL GINGERBREAD

  ½ **cup butter or margarine**
  ½ **cup sugar**
  2 **eggs**
  ¾ **cup molasses**
  2 **cups all-purpose flour**
  1 **teaspoon baking soda**
  ¼ **teaspoon salt**
  1 **teaspoon ground cinnamon**
  1 **teaspoon ground ginger**
  ¼ **teaspoon ground cloves**
  1 **cup buttermilk**
  ¾ **cup apricot preserves**
    Topping (recipe follows)

Cream butter; gradually add sugar, beating until light and fluffy. Add eggs, one at a time, beating well after each addition. Then stir in molasses.

Combine flour, soda, salt, cinnamon, ginger, and cloves; add to creamed mixture alternately with buttermilk, beginning and ending with flour mixture. Mix well after each addition.

Pour batter into a greased and floured 13- x 9- x 2-inch baking dish. Bake at 350° for 35 minutes. Spread apricot preserves over top; sprinkle with topping. Increase oven temperature to 400°, and bake an additional 10 minutes or until topping is browned and a wooden pick inserted in center comes out clean. Serve warm. Yield: 12 servings.

Topping:

2 tablespoons all-purpose flour
¼ cup plus 1 tablespoon butter or margarine, melted
½ cup firmly packed brown sugar
½ cup flaked coconut
½ cup chopped pecans

Combine all ingredients, mixing well. Yield: about 1¾ cups.

APRICOT BRANDY BREAD

1 cup chopped dried apricots
¼ cup plus 1 tablespoon apricot brandy
½ cup shortening
1 cup sugar
1 egg
2 cups all-purpose flour
1 teaspoon baking soda
¼ teaspoon salt
1 teaspoon ground cinnamon
½ teaspoon ground nutmeg
¼ teaspoon ground allspice
¼ teaspoon ground cloves
1 cup chopped pecans
1 cup applesauce

Combine apricots and brandy; cover and refrigerate overnight.

Cream shortening; gradually add sugar, beating well. Add egg, and mix well. Combine flour and next 6 ingredients; combine apricot mixture and pecans with 1 cup flour mixture. Toss apricot mixture well, to coat all pieces with flour; set aside. Add remaining flour mixture to creamed mixture alternately with applesauce, beginning and ending with flour mixture. Stir in reserved apricot mixture. Pour into a greased 9- x 5- x 3-inch loafpan; bake at 350° for 1 hour and 15 minutes or until a wooden pick inserted in center comes out clean. Cool loaf in pan 10 minutes; remove from pan, and cool completely on a wire rack. Yield: 1 loaf.

Note: Loaf may be frozen up to 3 months.

ORANGE UPSIDAISIES

½ cup sugar
⅓ cup butter or margarine
1 teaspoon grated orange rind
¾ cup orange juice
2 cups all-purpose flour
2½ teaspoons baking powder
¼ teaspoon salt
¾ cup milk
⅓ cup vegetable oil
2 tablespoons sugar
1 teaspoon ground cinnamon

Combine first 4 ingredients in a small saucepan; cook over low heat 10 minutes, stirring until sugar dissolves. Cool and pour into a 12- x 8- x 2-inch baking dish; set aside.

Combine flour, baking powder, and salt. Add milk and vegetable oil to flour mixture, mixing well.

Roll out on a floured surface to a 12- x 10-inch rectangle. Combine 2 tablespoons sugar and cinnamon, and sprinkle over dough. Roll up dough jellyroll fashion, beginning at long end. Cut into 12 equal slices, and arrange in prepared baking dish. Bake at 400° for 25 minutes. Invert immediately onto a serving plate, and serve warm. Yield: 1 dozen.

Beverages

VIENNESE CHOCOLATE

1 (6-ounce) package semisweet
    chocolate morsels
½ cup sugar
1 teaspoon grated orange rind
⅓ cup orange juice
½ teaspoon ground cinnamon
1 cup whipping cream, whipped
  Hot milk
  Cointreau or other orange-flavored
    liqueur (optional)
  Cinnamon sticks

Combine first 5 ingredients in a heavy saucepan. Cook over low heat, stirring constantly, until smooth. Remove from heat, and cool to lukewarm. Fold whipped cream into chocolate mixture; cover and refrigerate up to 1 week.

To serve, spoon 2 tablespoons chocolate mixture into each cup; add ⅔ cup hot milk and 1 ounce Cointreau, if desired, stirring until blended. Serve each with a cinnamon stick stirrer. Yield: enough to make about 20 cups hot chocolate.

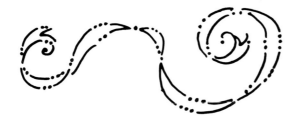

CRANBERRY BRACER

1 (16-ounce) can whole-berry
    cranberry sauce
1 (8-ounce) carton orange or
    vanilla-flavored yogurt
1 cup vanilla ice cream
¼ teaspoon ground cinnamon
⅛ teaspoon ground nutmeg
6 ice cubes
  Grape clusters (optional)

Combine first 6 ingredients in container of an electric blender. Process at high speed until smooth. Pour immediately into stemmed glasses; garnish glasses with grape clusters, if desired. Yield: 4 cups.

SPICY TOMATO FRAPPÉ

¼ cup finely chopped onion
1 tablespoon butter or margarine,
    melted
1 tablespoon lemon juice
2 teaspoons sugar
2 teaspoons Worcestershire sauce
2 cups Bloody Mary mix
2 cups tomato juice
  Celery stalks (optional)
  Cucumber slices (optional)

Sauté onion in butter until tender. Combine onion and next 4 ingredients in container of an electric blender; process until smooth. Add tomato juice; process at low speed until blended. Pour mixture into a 13- x 9- x 2-inch baking pan; cover and freeze 4 hours or until firm.

Remove mixture from freezer 20 minutes before serving. Break up mixture into chunks with a fork. Place one-fourth of mixture in container of an electric blender; process at low speed just until smooth (do not let mixture melt). Pour into glasses. Repeat process with remaining mixture; serve with celery stalks and cucumber slices, if desired. Yield: 4¼ cups.

Hot or frosty, these sublimely blended beverages are refreshing both in appearance and flavor. Clockwise from right: Spicy Tomato Frappé, Simple Syllabub, Viennese Chocolate, and Cranberry Bracer.

SIMPLE SYLLABUB

2 cups whipping cream
2 cups milk
½ cup cream sherry
¼ cup sugar
Dash of salt
Ground nutmeg

Combine cream, milk, sherry, sugar, and salt in a mixing bowl; beat at medium speed of an electric mixer until frothy. Pour into cups, and sprinkle with nutmeg. Yield: 4½ cups.

HUMMERS

¾ cup light rum
¼ cup plus 2 tablespoons Kahlúa or other coffee-flavored liqueur
1 pint vanilla or coffee ice cream
Ice cubes

Combine rum, Kahlúa, and ice cream in container of an electric blender; blend until smooth. Add ice cubes to the 5-cup line; blend until smooth. Serve immediately. Yield: 4 cups.

HOT APPLE RUM FOR TWO

2 teaspoons butter or margarine
2 teaspoons brown sugar
1¾ cups apple juice
Dash of ground cinnamon
Dash of salt
2 (3-inch) sticks cinnamon
2 tablespoons rum

Combine first 5 ingredients in a saucepan; bring to a boil. Place a cinnamon stick and 1 tablespoon rum into each serving cup; pour hot mixture into cups, stirring well. Yield: 1¾ cups.

RUM-CIDER TEA

1 quart water
4 (2-inch) strips orange rind
1 (3-inch) stick cinnamon
1 whole nutmeg
4 regular-size tea bags
2 cups apple cider or apple juice
¼ cup honey
¾ cup dark rum
Whipped cream (optional)
Ground nutmeg (optional)

Combine first 4 ingredients in a saucepan; bring to a boil. Add tea bags; cover, remove from heat, and brew 5 minutes.

Strain tea mixture; add apple cider, honey, and rum, stirring until blended. Pour hot tea mixture into mugs; top each with a dollop of whipped cream, and sprinkle with nutmeg, if desired. Yield: 7 cups.

CRANBERRY WINE PUNCH

3 cups fresh or frozen, thawed cranberries
2 cups orange juice, divided
½ cup sugar
6 whole cloves
6 whole allspice
1½ teaspoons ground cardamom
4 cups Chablis or other dry white wine
Twists of orange rind

Combine cranberries and 1 cup orange juice in container of an electric blender; process at high speed until cranberries are finely minced. Combine cranberry mixture, remaining 1 cup orange juice, sugar, cloves, allspice, and cardamom in a medium saucepan; bring to a boil. Cover, reduce heat, and simmer 30 minutes.

Strain mixture; discard cranberry pulp and spices. Return liquid to saucepan; add Chablis. Heat thoroughly (do not boil). Serve hot in mugs; garnish with twists of orange rind. Yield: about 6 cups.

Cakes and Pies

CHOCOLATE MOUSSE CAKE

- ½ cup unsalted butter
- 7 (1-ounce) squares semisweet chocolate
- 7 eggs, separated
- ¾ cup sugar
- 1 teaspoon vanilla extract
- ⅛ teaspoon cream of tartar
- ¼ cup sugar
  Whipped Cream Frosting
  Chocolate curls or grated chocolate
  Red candied cherry wedges

Combine butter and squares of chocolate in top of a double boiler; bring water to a boil. Reduce heat to low; cook until chocolate melts.

Combine egg yolks, ¾ cup sugar, and vanilla in a large mixing bowl; beat at high speed of an electric mixer until light and fluffy (about 5 minutes). Gradually add chocolate mixture, beating well; set aside.

Beat egg whites (at room temperature) and cream of tartar at high speed of an electric mixer 1 minute. Gradually add ¼ cup sugar, 1 tablespoon at a time, beating until stiff peaks form. Fold into chocolate mixture.

Pour three-fourths of batter into an ungreased 9-inch springform pan; bake at 325° for 35 minutes. Cover remaining batter, and refrigerate. Cool cake completely on a wire rack (cake will fall as it cools). Spread refrigerated batter over cake, and refrigerate overnight.

Remove sides of springform pan; spread or pipe Whipped Cream Frosting over top and sides using No. 5 or 6B large fluted tip. Garnish with chocolate curls and candied cherries. Yield: one 9-inch cake.

Whipped Cream Frosting:

- 1 cup whipping cream
- ⅓ cup sifted powdered sugar
- 1 teaspoon vanilla extract

Beat whipping cream until foamy; add sugar and vanilla, beating until soft peaks form. Yield: about 2 cups.

Crown this Chocolate Mousse Cake with piped-on Whipped Cream Frosting and bells formed with chocolate curls and slivers of candied cherries.

ORANGE CRUNCH CAKE

½ cup chopped pecans
½ cup sugar
⅓ cup fine, dry breadcrumbs
¼ teaspoon salt
⅓ cup butter, melted
¾ cup butter, softened
1⅓ cups sugar
3 eggs
⅔ cup milk
2 teaspoons vanilla extract
3 cups cake flour
2½ teaspoons baking powder
¼ teaspoon salt
1 tablespoon grated orange rind
Orange sauce (recipe follows)

Combine first 5 ingredients, mixing well; press mixture on bottom and 1 inch up sides of a greased 10-inch pan.

Cream ¾ cup butter; gradually add 1⅓ cups sugar, beating well. Add eggs, one at a time, beating well. Combine milk and vanilla; set aside. Combine flour, baking powder, and salt; add to creamed mixture alternately with milk mixture, beginning and ending with flour mixture. Stir in rind.

Pour batter into prepared pan; bake at 375° for 15 minutes. Reduce temperature to 350°, and bake an additional 45 minutes or until a wooden pick inserted in center comes out clean. Cool in pan 10 minutes; remove from pan, and spoon orange sauce over top. Yield: one 10-inch cake.

Orange Sauce:

½ cup sifted powdered sugar
1 teaspoon grated orange grind
2 tablespoons orange juice

Combine all ingredients, mixing well. Yield: about ¼ cup.

Clockwise from right: Chocolate Cream Pie, Pumpkin-Brandy Cheesecake, Chocolate Mousse Cake, and Peach Preserve Cake.

PUMPKIN-BRANDY CHEESECAKE

1½ cups gingersnap crumbs
1⅓ cups sliced almonds, toasted and divided
½ teaspoon ground cinnamon
⅓ cup butter or margarine, melted
4 (8-ounce) packages cream cheese, softened
1¼ cups sugar
1½ teaspoons pumpkin pie spice
½ teaspoon ground ginger
4 eggs
1 cup canned mashed pumpkin
¼ cup brandy
3 tablespoons half-and-half
1 (16-ounce) carton commercial sour cream
¼ cup sugar
2 tablespoons brandy
Green candied cherry wedges

Combine gingersnap crumbs, ⅓ cup almonds, and cinnamon, mixing well. Add butter, and blend well. Press evenly onto bottom of a 10-inch springform pan; bake at 425° for 10 minutes. Cool completely on a wire rack.

Beat cream cheese in a large mixing bowl until fluffy. Combine 1¼ cups sugar, pumpkin pie spice, and ginger; gradually add to cream cheese, and beat well. Add eggs, one at a time, beating well after each addition. Beat in pumpkin, ¼ cup brandy, and half-and-half. Pour into prepared pan; bake at 325° for 45 minutes. Turn off oven, but do not open oven door; let cake stand in oven 2 hours. Transfer cake to a wire rack, and cool completely.

Combine sour cream, ¼ cup sugar, and 2 tablespoons brandy; mix well. Pour mixture over cake, and spread evenly. Bake at 425° for 10 minutes. Cool completely on a wire rack. Cover the cheesecake, and refrigerate it overnight.

Remove sides of pan, and press ¾ cup toasted almonds on sides of cheesecake; arrange remaining almonds and candied cherries on top. Yield: 16 to 20 servings.

PEACH PRESERVE CAKE

¾ cup butter or margarine
1 cup sugar
3 eggs, separated
2 cups all-purpose flour
⅛ teaspoon salt
½ cup buttermilk
1 teaspoon baking soda
1 cup peach preserves
Orange Frosting
4 candied pineapple slices, halved
8 walnut halves
8 candied cherries

Cream butter in a large mixing bowl; gradually add sugar, beating until light and fluffy. Add egg yolks, one at a time, beating well after each addition. Combine flour and salt. Combine buttermilk and soda; add to creamed mixture alternately with flour mixture, beginning and ending with flour mixture. Stir in peach preserves.

Beat egg whites (at room temperature) until stiff peaks form; fold into batter. Pour batter into 3 greased and floured 8-inch round cakepans. Bake at 350° for 25 to 27 minutes or until a wooden pick inserted in center comes out clean. Cool in pans 10 minutes; remove from pans, and cool completely on wire racks. Spread Orange Frosting between layers and on top and sides of cake. Arrange candied pineapple, walnuts, and cherries on cake as desired. Yield: one 3-layer cake.

Orange Frosting:

2 cups sugar
1 cup milk
1 cup coconut
1 cup chopped walnuts
1 orange, seeded, ground, and
drained
1 (8-ounce) can crushed pineapple,
drained

Combine sugar and milk in a Dutch oven. Bring to a boil over low heat, stirring constantly until sugar dissolves; cook to hard ball stage (260°). Remove from heat, and beat at high speed of an electric mixer 5 minutes or until smooth and creamy; stir in remaining ingredients. Yield: enough frosting for one 3-layer cake.

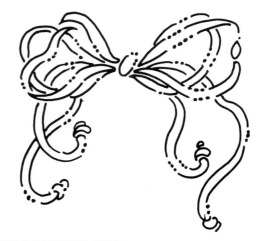

RICH FRUITCAKE

1 (15-ounce) package golden raisins
¼ pound currants
½ cup dark rum
1 (16-ounce) package candied yellow
pineapple, chopped
1 (8-ounce) package candied red
cherries, halved
1 (4-ounce) package candied citron,
finely chopped
1 cup chopped almonds
1 cup chopped pecans
2 ounces candied lemon peel, finely
chopped
2 ounces candied orange peel, finely
chopped
2 cups all-purpose flour, divided
½ teaspoon baking soda
½ teaspoon ground mace
½ teaspoon ground cinnamon
½ cup butter, softened
1 cup sugar
1 cup firmly packed brown sugar
5 eggs
1 tablespoon milk
1 teaspoon almond extract
½ cup dark rum

Combine raisins, currants, and ½ cup rum in a small bowl; cover mixture and let stand overnight.

Combine raisin mixture and next 7 ingredients in a large mixing bowl; dredge with ½ cup flour, stirring to coat well. Set aside. Combine remaining 1½ cups flour with soda, mace, and cinnamon; set aside.

Cream butter in a large mixing bowl; gradually add sugars, beating well. Add eggs, one at a time, beating well after each addition. Stir in milk and almond extract. Add flour mixture, and beat well. Pour over candied fruit mixture, and stir until fruit is evenly coated.

Pour batter into a brown paper-lined and greased 10-inch tube pan. Bake at 275° for 3 hours and 15 minutes or until a wooden pick inserted in center comes out clean. Cool 30 minutes; remove from pan, and cool completely on a wire rack. Wrap cake in cheesecloth, and pour remaining ½ cup rum evenly over top. Seal in an airtight container, and allow to age at least two weeks before serving. Yield: one 10-inch cake.

TRIPLE CROWN CAKE

- **1 cup butter, softened**
- **2 cups sugar**
- **4 eggs, separated**
- **2⅔ cups sifted cake flour**
- **1 tablespoon plus 1 teaspoon baking powder**
- **⅛ teaspoon salt**
- **1 cup milk**
- **1 teaspoon vanilla extract**
- **Golden Walnut Filling**
- **Fluff Frosting**

Cream the butter in a large mixing bowl; gradually add the sugar, beating well. Add the egg yolks, one at a time, beating well after each addition.

Combine flour, baking powder, and salt; add to creamed mixture alternately with milk, beginning and ending with flour mixture. Stir in vanilla.

Beat egg whites (at room temperature) at high speed of an electric mixer until stiff peaks form. Fold into cake mixture.

Pour batter into 3 greased and floured 9-inch round cakepans. Bake at 375° for 20 to 25 minutes or until a wooden pick inserted in center comes out clean. Cool in pans 10 minutes; remove from pans, and cool completely on wire racks.

Spread Golden Walnut Filling between layers; spread top and sides with Fluff Frosting. Yield: one 3-layer cake.

Golden Walnut Filling:

- **2 cups golden raisins, minced**
- **½ cup sugar**
- **3 tablespoons cornstarch**
- **1 tablespoon grated orange rind**
- **½ cup orange juice**
- **½ cup water**
- **½ cup chopped walnuts**
- **2 to 3 tablespoons bourbon**

Combine first 6 ingredients in a heavy saucepan, mixing well. Cook over low heat, stirring constantly, about 5 minutes or until thickened. Cool completely; stir in remaining ingredients. Yield: enough filling for one 3-layer cake.

Fluff Frosting:

- **1 cup light corn syrup**
- **Pinch of salt**
- **2 egg whites**
- **¼ cup sifted powdered sugar**
- **1 teaspoon vanilla extract**

Combine syrup and salt in a small saucepan; bring to a boil.

Beat egg whites (at room temperature) at high speed of an electric mixer until soft peaks form. With electric mixer running, gradually add hot syrup mixture in a slow, steady stream. Gradually add sugar, one tablespoon at a time, beating until frosting is thick enough to spread. Beat in vanilla. Yield: enough frosting for one 3-layer cake.

CHOCOLATE CREAM PIE WITH CHERRY SAUCE

1½ cups whipping cream
 3 (1-ounce) squares unsweetened chocolate, coarsely chopped
¾ cup sugar
 2 tablespoons cornstarch
⅛ teaspoon salt
 2 eggs, beaten
1½ teaspoons vanilla extract
 1 unbaked 9-inch pastry shell
   Sifted powdered sugar (optional)
   Cherry Sauce

Combine whipping cream and chocolate in a heavy saucepan; cook over low heat, stirring constantly, until mixture is smooth; set aside.

Combine sugar, cornstarch, and salt in a medium bowl, mixing well; stir in eggs, vanilla, and chocolate mixture. Pour into pastry shell; bake at 400° for 35 minutes. Cool completely on a wire rack. Place an 8-inch stencil on pie; sprinkle powdered sugar over it. Remove stencil. Serve with Cherry Sauce. Yield: one 9-inch pie.

Cherry Sauce:

¼ cup brandy
 1 teaspoon cornstarch
 1 (16-ounce) can cherry pie filling

Combine brandy and cornstarch in a small saucepan, stirring until smooth; add pie filling, and cook over medium heat, stirring constantly, until mixture is clear and thickened. Yield: about 2¼ cups.

SWEET POTATO PRALINE PIE

- ½ cup butter or margarine
- 1 cup chopped pecans
- 1 cup cooked, mashed sweet potatoes
- 3 eggs, beaten
- ½ cup firmly packed brown sugar
- 1 cup dark corn syrup
- 1 teaspoon pumpkin pie spice
- 1½ teaspoons vanilla extract
- 2 tablespoons bourbon (optional)
- 1 unbaked 9-inch pastry shell
  Whipped cream

Melt butter in a large, heavy saucepan; add pecans, and cook over low heat, stirring constantly, until butter is golden brown and pecans are toasted. Remove from heat; stir in next 7 ingredients, mixing well.

Pour mixture into pastry shell. Bake at 425° for 10 minutes. Reduce temperature to 325°, and bake an additional 45 minutes or until set. Cool on a wire rack; top with whipped cream. Yield: one 9-inch pie.

CHEDDAR-APPLE PIE

- 1 cup sugar
- 2½ tablespoons all-purpose flour
- ½ teaspoon ground cinnamon
- 1 teaspoon grated lemon rind
- ⅛ teaspoon salt
- 6 medium cooking apples, peeled, cored, and thinly sliced
- 1 unbaked 9-inch pastry shell
- ½ cup all-purpose flour
- ¼ cup sugar
- ½ cup (2 ounces) shredded Cheddar cheese
- ¼ cup butter or margarine, melted
  Rum Sauce

Combine first 5 ingredients in a large bowl; add apples, and toss gently to coat apples. Pour into pastry shell.

Combine next 4 ingredients, mixing well; sprinkle over apples. Bake at 400° for 40 minutes. Serve with Rum Sauce. Yield: one 9-inch pie.

Rum Sauce:

- ⅓ cup sugar
- 2 teaspoons cornstarch
- ⅛ teaspoon salt
- ⅔ cup apple juice
- 2 teaspoons butter or margarine
- 1 tablespoon dark rum
- ½ teaspoon vanilla extract

Combine sugar, cornstarch, salt, and apple juice in a small saucepan. Cook over medium heat, stirring constantly, until sugar dissolves and mixture is clear and thickened. Remove from heat, and stir in butter, rum, and vanilla. Yield: about 1 cup.

FRENCH RAISIN PIE

- 3 eggs, beaten
- ½ cup butter or margarine, melted
- ¾ cup sugar
- 1 teaspoon vinegar
- 1 teaspoon vanilla extract
- ½ teaspoon ground cinnamon
- ½ teaspoon ground allspice
  Dash of salt
- ½ cup chopped black walnuts
- ½ cup raisins
- 1 unbaked 8-inch pastry shell
  Whipped cream

Combine first 10 ingredients; mix well, and pour into pastry shell. Bake at 300° for 50 minutes. Serve warm or chilled with whipped cream. Yield: one 8-inch pie.

Cookies and Candies

VANILLA BEAN COOKIES

1 vanilla bean, finely diced
1 cup sifted powdered sugar
2 cups butter, softened
1 cup sugar
1 teaspoon vanilla extract
4 cups all-purpose flour
2¼ cups ground pecans (about ½ pound)

Combine vanilla bean and powdered sugar in an airtight container; let stand three days.

Cream butter; gradually add sugar, beating well. Stir in vanilla. Add flour and pecans, mixing well. Chill dough overnight. Remove dough from refrigerator, and let stand until soft enough to roll. Roll dough to ⅛-inch thickness on a floured surface; cut into desired shapes. Place cookies on lightly greased cookie sheets. Bake at 350° for 12 minutes; transfer to wire racks. Sift vanilla bean-flavored powdered sugar over cookies while warm. Yield: about 6 dozen (2¼-inch) cookies.

GINGER COOKIES

¾ cup shortening
1 cup sugar
1 egg
¼ cup molasses
2 cups all-purpose flour
2 teaspoons baking soda
½ teaspoon salt
1 tablespoon ground ginger
1 teaspoon ground cinnamon
About ⅓ cup sugar

Cream shortening; gradually add 1 cup sugar, beating until light and fluffy. Beat in egg and molasses. Combine next 5 ingredients; add to mixture, mixing well.

Shape dough into 1-inch balls, and roll in ⅓ cup sugar. Place 2 inches apart on ungreased cookie sheets; bake at 350° for 8 to 10 minutes. Cool on cookie sheets 5 minutes; transfer to wire racks using a spatula, and cool completely. Yield: 7 dozen.

APRICOT GRANOLA BARS

3 cups regular oats, uncooked
½ cup sunflower kernels
½ cup firmly packed light brown sugar
½ cup apricot preserves
½ cup butter or margarine
1 cup crushed bran cereal
¾ cup raisins
¾ cup candy-coated milk chocolate pieces

Combine oats and sunflower kernels in a jellyroll pan; bake at 350° for 20 minutes or until lightly toasted, stirring every 5 minutes. Cool.

Combine sugar, preserves, and butter in a heavy saucepan; cook over medium heat, stirring occasionally, until mixture reaches soft ball stage (234°).

Combine oat mixture, cereal, raisins, and chocolate pieces in a large bowl; pour hot sugar mixture over oat mixture, and mix well. Press mixture into a greased and floured 13- x 9- x 2-inch baking pan; bake at 350° for 12 to 15 minutes. Cool completely on a wire rack; cut into bars. Yield: 2 dozen.

Splurge on sweets for the holidays. In tray, left to right: Mint Chocolate Snaps, star-shaped Vanilla Bean Cookies, White Chocolate Crunch, Chocolate Marbles, and Chocolate Chip Toffee Grahams. Center: Apricot Granola Bars in glass basket, Ginger Cookies in ginger jar, and Chocolate Caramels in top tier of server.

MINT CHOCOLATE SNAPS

1 (6-ounce) package semisweet
    chocolate morsels
½ cup plus 1½ tablespoons
    shortening
¾ cup sugar
1 egg
¼ cup light corn syrup
1 teaspoon peppermint extract
1 teaspoon vanilla extract
2 cups all-purpose flour
1 teaspoon baking soda
¼ teaspoon salt
¼ cup crushed peppermint candy
    About ⅓ cup sugar

Melt chocolate morsels in top of a double boiler. Remove from heat, and set aside.

Cream shortening; gradually add ¾ cup sugar, beating until light and fluffy. Beat in melted chocolate. Add egg, corn syrup, and flavorings; beat well. Combine flour, soda, and salt; stir into chocolate mixture. Stir in peppermint candy.

Shape dough into 1-inch balls, and roll in ⅓ cup sugar. Place balls 2 inches apart on ungreased cookie sheets; bake at 350° for 12 to 15 minutes. Cool on cookie sheets 5 minutes; transfer to wire racks, and cool completely. Yield: about 7 dozen.

CHOCOLATE CHIP TOFFEE GRAHAMS

11 whole graham crackers (4½- x 2¼
    inches), broken into squares
1 cup butter or margarine
1 cup sugar
1 teaspoon ground cinnamon
½ cup finely chopped pecans
1 (6-ounce) package semisweet
    chocolate mini-morsels

Arrange graham cracker squares in a single layer in a 15- x 10- x 1-inch jellyroll pan. Combine butter and sugar in a saucepan. Bring to a boil over medium heat, stirring constantly until butter melts; boil 2 minutes. Remove from heat, and stir in cinnamon and pecans. Pour mixture evenly over graham crackers; spread to edges of pan, covering graham crackers completely. Bake at 350° for 10 to 12 minutes.

Remove from oven, and sprinkle with chocolate morsels. Cool in pan 5 minutes; carefully separate and transfer cookies to waxed paper-lined cookie sheets using a spatula. Refrigerate until chocolate hardens. Store cookies, layered between pieces of waxed paper, in airtight containers in refrigerator. Yield: 22 cookies.

LEBKUCHEN BARS

1 egg, beaten
1 cup firmly packed brown sugar
½ cup molasses
½ cup honey
3½ cups all-purpose flour
½ teaspoon baking soda
⅛ teaspoon salt
1 teaspoon ground cinnamon
1 teaspoon ground nutmeg
1 teaspoon ground cloves
¾ cup chopped candied cherries
½ cup slivered almonds, toasted
    Lemon icing (recipe follows)

Combine egg and brown sugar in a large mixing bowl; mix well. Stir in molasses and honey, and set aside.

Combine dry ingredients. Combine 1 cup flour mixture, cherries, and almonds, tossing to coat; set aside. Add remaining flour mixture to molasses mixture, stirring well; fold in cherries and almonds.

Pat dough into a greased 15- x 10- x 1-inch jellyroll pan. Bake at 300° for 40 minutes. Cool on wire rack, and frost with lemon icing; cut into bars. Yield: 35 bars.

Lemon Icing:

- 1 egg white, beaten
- 2 cups sifted powdered sugar
- ½ teaspoon grated lemon rind
- 1 tablespoon lemon juice
- ⅛ teaspoon salt

Combine all ingredients, mixing well. Yield: about ¾ cup.

WHITE CHOCOLATE CRUNCH

- 2 pounds white chocolate, coarsely chopped
- 2 tablespoons shortening
- 1½ cups oven-toasted rice cereal
- 1½ cups crunchy-sweet peanut butter cereal
- 1½ cups miniature marshmallows
- 1 cup chopped pecans

Melt white chocolate and shortening in top of a double boiler over hot water; combine white chocolate mixture with remaining ingredients, mixing well. Drop by heaping teaspoonfuls onto waxed paper. Let cool completely; store in an airtight container. Yield: about 5 dozen.

CHOCOLATE MARBLES

- 2 cups (9½ ounces) amaretti almond cookie crumbs
- ¾ cup butter, softened
- ⅓ cup amaretto
- 1 (8-ounce) package semisweet chocolate

Combine first 3 ingredients, mixing well; chill. Shape mixture into ¾-inch balls.

Place chocolate in top of a double boiler; bring water to a boil. Reduce heat to low; cook until chocolate melts. Dip each ball into melted chocolate; refrigerate 30 minutes or until chocolate hardens. Store in airtight container in refrigerator. Yield: about 5 dozen.

EGGNOG CANDY

- 2 cups commercial eggnog
- 4 cups sugar
- ¼ cup light corn syrup
- ¼ teaspoon salt
- ¼ cup butter
- 1 cup diced candied fruit
- 1 cup chopped pecans

Combine eggnog, sugar, corn syrup, and salt in a Dutch oven; cook over low heat, stirring frequently, until mixture reaches soft ball stage (234°). Cool to lukewarm; add butter, and beat until mixture is no longer shiny (about 5 minutes). Stir in fruit and pecans. Spread in a buttered 8-inch square pan. Cool and cut into squares. Yield: 25 squares.

CHOCOLATE CARAMELS

- 3 cups firmly packed light brown sugar
- 3 tablespoons all-purpose flour
- 1½ cups molasses
- ¾ cup butter or margarine
- 6 (1-ounce) squares unsweetened chocolate
- 1½ cups milk
- 1½ teaspoons vanilla extract
- ⅓ cup sliced almonds, toasted

Combine first 4 ingredients in a heavy saucepan. Bring to a boil, stirring constantly; reduce heat, and cook 5 minutes. Add chocolate and milk; stir until chocolate melts. Cook over medium heat, stirring frequently, until mixture reaches soft ball stage (238°). Remove from heat, and stir in vanilla.

Pour mixture into a buttered 9-inch square pan; sprinkle with almonds. Cover and chill overnight; cut into squares. Store in refrigerator. Yield: 3 dozen.

Gift Ideas

SPICED YEAST DOUGHNUTS

    1 package dry yeast
    ¼ cup warm water (105° to 115°)
    ¾ cup milk
    ¼ cup sugar or honey
    ¾ teaspoon salt
    ¼ cup butter or margarine
    ½ teaspoon ground cinnamon
    ½ teaspoon ground nutmeg
    4 cups all-purpose flour, divided
    1 egg, beaten
      Vegetable oil
      Sifted powdered sugar

Dissolve yeast in water in a large mixing bowl; let stand 5 minutes.

Combine milk, sugar, salt, butter, and spices in a small saucepan. Cook over medium-low heat, stirring until butter melts. Cool to lukewarm (105° to 115°). Stir milk mixture and 2 cups flour into yeast mixture; beat until smooth. Add egg and remaining 2 cups flour, mixing to form a soft dough.

Turn dough out onto a floured surface, and knead 5 to 8 minutes or until smooth and elastic. Place in a well-greased bowl, turning to grease top. Cover and let rise in a warm place (85°), free from drafts, 1 hour or until doubled in bulk.

Punch dough down; let rest 10 minutes. Place dough on a lightly floured surface; roll to ½-inch thickness. Cut with a floured 2½-inch doughnut cutter.

Place doughnuts several inches apart on greased baking sheets; cover and let rise in a warm place 20 to 25 minutes.

Gifts of prettily packaged, home-cooked goodies will warm the hearts of friends and neighbors. Clockwise from back: Pickled Dried Apricots, Spiced Yeast Doughnuts, Fruited Cranberry Relish, and Cream Cheese Rounds.

Heat 2 inches of oil to 375°; cook 3 or 4 doughnuts at a time. Cook about 1 minute or until golden on one side; turn and cook other side about 1 minute. Drain on absorbent towels. Sprinkle with powdered sugar. Store in airtight container up to 2 days. Yield: about 1½ dozen.

PICKLED DRIED APRICOTS

    1 (6-ounce) package dried apricot
        halves
    2 cups water
    1 cup firmly packed brown sugar
    3 tablespoons vinegar
   12 whole cloves
    1 (3-inch) stick cinnamon
    ¼ teaspoon whole mustard seeds

Place apricots and water in a heavy saucepan; cook, uncovered, over low heat 10 minutes. Add remaining ingredients, and simmer 25 minutes. Cool; store in a jar in refrigerator up to 2 weeks. Yield: 1⅓ cups.

FRUITED CRANBERRY RELISH

    2 (15¼-ounce) cans pineapple
        chunks, undrained
    2 (12-ounce) packages (about 6 cups)
        fresh cranberries
    2 cups sugar
    2 cups raisins
    1 tablespoon minced crystallized
        ginger
    ¼ teaspoon salt
    ½ teaspoon ground allspice

Drain pineapple, reserving ½ cup juice. Combine reserved juice, cranberries, and next 5 ingredients in a Dutch oven; bring to a boil. Cover and simmer 10 minutes. Stir in pineapple chunks; simmer, uncovered, an additional 5 minutes. Chill. Serve with roasted meats. Relish will keep up to 2 weeks in the refrigerator. Yield: about 2 quarts.

CREAM CHEESE ROUNDS

1 cup butter, softened
2 (3-ounce) packages cream cheese, softened
2 cups all-purpose flour
2 tablespoons sugar
2 teaspoons baking powder
Raspberry or apricot preserves

Combine butter and cream cheese in a large mixing bowl; beat at high speed of an electric mixer until smooth. Combine flour, sugar, and baking powder; beat into cream cheese mixture. Shape dough into a ball; wrap in plastic wrap, and chill until firm.

Roll dough on a floured surface to ⅛-inch thickness. Cut with a 2¼-inch round cutter, and place on greased cookie sheets. Make an indentation in center of each round with back of a spoon. Place 1 teaspoon preserves in center of each round. Bake at 400° for 10 to 12 minutes. Store in refrigerator in airtight container up to 1 week. Yield: about 3½ dozen.

MORAVIAN SUGAR CAKE

1 package dry yeast
½ teaspoon sugar
¼ cup warm water (105° to 115°)
1 cup unsalted hot mashed potatoes
1 cup sugar
½ cup shortening
¼ cup butter
1 teaspoon salt
2 eggs, beaten
5 to 6 cups all-purpose flour
1 cup cold butter, cut into ⅛-inch slices
1½ cups plus 2 tablespoons firmly packed brown sugar
Ground cinnamon

Dissolve yeast and ½ teaspoon sugar in water; let stand 5 minutes.

Combine potatoes, 1 cup sugar, shortening, ¼ cup butter, and salt in a large bowl; stir until shortening melts. Then stir in yeast mixture.

Cover mixing bowl, and let dough rise in a warm place (85°), free from drafts, 1½ hours or until spongy.

Stir in eggs and enough flour to make a soft dough that leaves sides of bowl. Shape dough into a ball; place in a well-greased bowl, turning to grease top. Cover and let rise in a warm place (85°), free from drafts, two hours or until doubled in bulk.

Turn dough out onto a lightly floured surface, and knead 5 minutes or until smooth and elastic. Divide dough in half; pat evenly into two greased 13- x 9- x 2-inch baking pans. Cover and let rise in a warm place (85°), free from drafts, 1½ hours or until doubled in bulk.

Press slices of butter into dough at about ½-inch intervals in rows. Top each slice of butter with about 1 teaspoon brown sugar. Sprinkle cinnamon over entire surface. Bake at 375° for 20 minutes or until golden brown. Store in airtight containers up to 4 days. Yield: two 13- x 9-inch cakes.

Note: Cake may be frozen; remove from freezer, and heat at 350° until warm.

PINEAPPLE-CHERRY SAUCE

¼ cup brandy
2 tablespoons minced crystallized ginger
1 (20-ounce) can pineapple chunks, undrained
1 tablespoon cornstarch
¼ cup honey
½ teaspoon ground cinnamon
⅛ teaspoon ground cloves
1 (16-ounce) can pitted dark sweet cherries, drained

Combine brandy and ginger in a small bowl; let stand 1 hour.

Drain pineapple, reserving juice and pineapple separately. Combine reserved juice and next 4 ingredients in a medium saucepan; cook over medium heat, stirring constantly, until thickened. Stir in reserved pineapple chunks, cherries, and ginger mixture; heat thoroughly. Serve hot or cold over pound cake, waffles, or ice cream. Refrigerate up to 2 weeks. Yield: about 4½ cups.

CASHEW-HONEY BUTTER

1 cup dry-roasted cashews
2 tablespoons vegetable oil
1 tablespoon honey

Place cashews in container of an electric blender; process at low speed until finely chopped. Add oil and honey; process at high speed until smooth. Serve on crackers or bread. Store in refrigerator up to 1 month. Yield: ¾ cup.

SANGRIA JELLY

6 cups sugar
3 cups Burgundy
2 tablespoons grated orange rind
½ cup orange juice
1 tablespoon plus 1 teaspoon
    Cointreau or other
    orange-flavored liqueur
2 (3-ounce) packages liquid fruit
    pectin

Combine first 5 ingredients in a large Dutch oven; bring to a boil. Boil mixture 1 to 2 minutes, stirring frequently. Remove mixture from heat; stir in fruit pectin. Skim off foam with a metal spoon. Quickly pour jelly into hot sterilized jars, leaving ½-inch headspace; cover at once with metal lids, and screw bands tight. Process in boiling-water bath 5 minutes. Store in cool, dry place up to 1 year. Yield: 6 to 7 half-pints.

PECANS OLÉ

1 egg white
1 tablespoon prepared mustard
½ teaspoon red pepper
2 cups pecan halves
½ cup grated Parmesan cheese
1 teaspoon paprika

Combine first 3 ingredients in a large bowl; beat well. Add pecans; stir well. Combine cheese and paprika; add to pecans, and toss until pecans are evenly coated.

Spread pecan mixture in a single layer in a greased 15- x 10- x 1-inch jellyroll pan. Bake at 300° for 25 minutes, stirring every 10 minutes. Remove to waxed paper while still hot; cool completely. Store in an airtight container in refrigerator up to 2 weeks. Yield: 2½ cups.

CARROT PICKLES

3 pounds baby carrots
2 cups vinegar (5% acidity)
1½ cups water
1 cup sugar
1 teaspoon salt
1 (3-inch) stick cinnamon
1 tablespoon mixed pickling spices

Scrub carrots; cover and cook in boiling water 20 minutes or until tender. Drain carrots, and remove skins.

Combine vinegar, 1½ cups water, sugar, and salt in a saucepan. Tie cinnamon stick and pickling spices in a cheesecloth bag; add to vinegar mixture. Bring mixture to a boil, and boil 5 to 8 minutes. Remove spice bag.

Pack carrots in hot sterilized jars, leaving ¼-inch headspace (cut large carrots into pieces, if necessary). Pour boiling hot syrup over carrots. Cover at once with metal lids, and screw bands tight. Process in boiling-water bath 30 minutes. Store in cool, dry place up to 1 year. Yield: 3 pints.

Party Fare

CHUTNEY SPREAD

1 (8-ounce) package cream cheese, softened
1 (9-ounce) jar chutney
½ cup chopped green onions with tops
½ cup coarsely chopped, dry-roasted peanuts
½ cup flaked coconut
 Candied cherry wedges

Spread cream cheese into a 7½-inch-diameter circle on a serving plate. Spread chutney over cream cheese; then top with rings of green onion and peanuts, and sprinkle coconut in center. Arrange candied cherry wedges like a flower on coconut. Serve immediately or refrigerate up to 1 hour. Serve with crackers or toast cut with Christmas-shaped cookie cutters. Yield: 1 (7½-inch) cheese round.

To accompany Chutney Spread, stamp out festive shapes from bread with cookie cutters. Butter bread and toast to a golden brown.

CHICKEN WITH CHERRY SAUCE

3 pounds chicken drummettes
2 cups buttermilk
¾ cup all-purpose flour
¾ cup crushed corn flakes cereal
¾ teaspoon seasoned salt
½ teaspoon red pepper
 Vegetable oil
 Cherry Sauce

Combine chicken and buttermilk; cover and refrigerate 4 hours.

Combine next 4 ingredients; mix well. Drain chicken pieces, and dredge in flour mixture. Heat 2 inches oil to 325° in a large, heavy skillet; fry chicken, in 2 batches, 10 minutes or until browned and cooked. Drain on paper towels. Serve with Cherry Sauce. Yield: about 4 dozen.

Cherry Sauce:

½ cup red wine vinegar
½ cup firmly packed brown sugar
1½ teaspoons dried whole basil
¼ teaspoon ground ginger
⅛ teaspoon ground cloves
1 (10-ounce) jar cherry preserves
1 cup Burgundy
3 tablespoons cornstarch

Combine first 5 ingredients in a small saucepan; bring to a boil, stirring constantly until sugar melts. Reduce heat, and simmer 5 minutes. Add preserves, and stir until melted and blended.

Combine Burgundy and cornstarch, mixing well; stir into preserves mixture. Cook, stirring constantly, until mixture is clear and thickened. Serve sauce warm with chicken. Yield: 2½ cups.

Party food, clockwise from back: Shrimp Dip, Festive Ham Spread, Chutney Spread, and Chicken with Cherry Sauce.

118

FESTIVE HAM SPREAD

    4 cups finely chopped ham
    1 (8-ounce) package cream cheese,
        divided and softened
    ¾ cup mayonnaise or salad dressing,
        divided
    ½ cup sliced green onions
    ¼ cup sweet pickle relish
        Sliced almonds, toasted
        Sliced green onion tops

Combine ham, 4 ounces cream cheese, ½ cup mayonnaise, onion, and relish in a small mixing bowl; mix well. Chill. Combine remaining 4 ounces cream cheese and ¼ cup mayonnaise; chill.

Spoon mixture onto serving plate, and shape into a tree. Spread cream cheese mixture on top and sides of ham mixture. Arrange sliced almonds and green onion tops attractively on tree. Serve with crackers. Yield: 4¼ cups.

SHRIMP DIP

    3 cups water
    1 pound fresh medium shrimp
    2 (8-ounce) packages cream cheese,
        cubed and softened
    3 tomatoes, peeled, seeded, and
        chopped
    2 green onions, chopped
    1 chile pepper, chopped
    ¼ teaspoon chili powder
    ¼ teaspoon paprika
        Green onion fan
    1 whole pimiento, cut with
        flower-shaped cookie cutter

Bring water to a boil; add shrimp. Reduce heat and simmer 3 minutes or until shrimp are done. Drain well; rinse with cold water.

Chill. Peel, devein, and chop shrimp; set aside.

Combine next 6 ingredients in a heavy saucepan; cook over low heat, stirring occasionally, until cheese melts. Stir in shrimp; cook just until shrimp are hot. Spoon into serving dish, and garnish with green onion fan and pimiento flower. Serve hot with breadsticks or chips. Yield: about 5 cups.

SHRIMP-STUFFED CHERRY TOMATOES

    3 cups water
    ¾ pound fresh medium shrimp
    1 pint (about 20) cherry tomatoes
    2 slices bacon, cooked and
        crumbled
    ⅓ cup commercial sour cream
    2 tablespoons mayonnaise
    ¼ teaspoon onion salt
        Fresh parsley sprigs

Bring water to a boil; add shrimp. Reduce heat, and simmer 3 minutes or until done. Drain well; rinse with cold water. Chill. Peel, devein, and finely chop shrimp. Set aside.

Wash tomatoes, and cut a thin slice from top of each; carefully scoop out pulp, leaving shells intact. Invert shells on paper towels, and let drain 30 minutes.

Combine shrimp and next 4 ingredients in a small bowl; mix well. Spoon shrimp mixture into tomato shells. Garnish with parsley. Yield: about 20.

MINI ORANGE-GLAZED SPARERIBS

    4 pounds spareribs
    1 (6-ounce) can frozen orange juice
        concentrate, thawed and
        undiluted
    1½ teaspoons Worcestershire sauce
    ½ teaspoon garlic salt
    ⅛ teaspoon pepper

Have butcher cut rack of ribs in half horizontally; cut ribs into appetizer-size servings. Place in a large Dutch oven. Add enough water to cover ribs; bring to a boil. Cover, reduce heat, and simmer 1 hour. Drain ribs, and place in a large shallow roasting pan; set aside.

Combine remaining ingredients; mix well. Brush ribs with sauce. Bake, uncovered, at 325° for 30 to 40 minutes, basting and turning occasionally. Yield: about 16 appetizer servings.

DRIED BEEF-CHEESE LOG

- 1 (8-ounce) package cream cheese, softened
- ½ cup (2 ounces) shredded sharp Cheddar cheese
- ½ cup finely chopped pimiento-stuffed olives
- 1 (2½-ounce) jar dried beef, finely chopped

Combine cheese and olives; mix well. Chill until firm. Shape mixture into a 10-inch log; roll log in chopped beef. Serve with crackers. Yield: one cheese log.

BAKED GOUDA IN PASTRY

- 1 (17¼-ounce) package frozen puff pastry
- 1 cup finely chopped pecans, divided
- 2 (10-ounce) rounds Gouda cheese, rind removed

Thaw 1 sheet pastry according to package directions; reserve second sheet in freezer for another use. Cut thawed pastry sheet in half, and roll out each half on a lightly floured surface to an 8-inch square. Sprinkle ¼ cup pecans in center of each pastry square. Place cheese rounds over pecans,

and sprinkle ¼ cup pecans over each cheese round. Bring up 4 corners of each pastry square to meet at top center; twist corners, and mold pastry edges over cheese to completely enclose cheese. Place cheese pastries in a lightly greased baking pan, and refrigerate until ready to bake.

Bake cheese at 400° for 25 minutes or until pastry is puffed and golden brown. Transfer to serving plates, and serve immediately. Yield: 12 appetizer servings.

TOASTED MUSHROOM ROLLS

- ¾ pound fresh mushrooms, finely chopped
- ¼ cup plus 2 tablespoons butter or margarine
- ¼ cup all-purpose flour
- 1 teaspoon salt
- 1½ cups half-and-half
- 3 tablespoons minced chives
- 1½ teaspoons lemon juice
- 2 (1-pound) loaves sliced sandwich bread, crust removed
- ½ cup butter or margarine, melted

Sauté mushrooms in butter in a heavy saucepan 5 minutes or until tender. Add flour and salt, stirring until smooth; cook 1 minute, stirring constantly. Gradually add half-and-half; cook over medium heat, stirring constantly, until mixture is thickened and bubbly. Stir in chives and lemon juice; set aside.

Roll bread slices with a rolling pin to make them thin. Spread 2 teaspoons mushroom mixture on each bread slice, and roll up, jellyroll fashion. Place rolls, seam side down, on greased baking sheets; brush with melted butter. Bake at 400° for 15 minutes. Serve hot. Yield: about 2½ to 3 dozen.

CURRIED PARTY MIX

    3 cups bite-size crispy corn cereal
       squares
    3 cups bite-size crispy wheat cereal
       squares
 1½ cups cashews
    1 cup flaked coconut
  ½ cup butter or margarine, melted
    1 to 1½ teaspoons curry powder
       Dash of red pepper
    1 cup dried banana chips
    1 cup raisins

Combine first 4 ingredients in a large bowl; combine butter, curry powder, and red pepper, and pour over cereal mixture. Toss to coat evenly. Spread mixture in an ungreased jellyroll pan. Bake at 250° for 45 minutes, stirring every 15 minutes; stir in banana chips and raisins during last 15 minutes of baking. Cool completely; store in an airtight container. Yield: 10 cups.

COLORFUL CHEESE BALL

    2 (8-ounce) packages cream cheese,
       softened
    2 cups (8 ounces) shredded Cheddar
       cheese
    1 tablespoon chopped pimiento
    1 tablespoon chopped green pepper
    1 tablespoon minced onion
    2 teaspoons Worcestershire sauce
    1 teaspoon lemon juice
       Dash of salt
       Red pepper to taste
       Chopped pecans

Combine all ingredients except pecans; mix well. Chill at least 1 hour. Shape into a ball, and coat with pecans. Yield: 1 cheese ball.

PECAN CRISPIES

  ½ cup butter or margarine, softened
  ½ cup shortening
    2 cups firmly packed brown sugar
    2 eggs
 2½ cups all-purpose flour
  ½ teaspoon baking soda
  ¼ teaspoon salt
    1 cup chopped pecans

Cream butter and shortening; gradually add sugar, beating until light and fluffy. Add eggs, beating well. Combine flour, soda, and salt; add to creamed mixture, beating well. Stir in pecans.

Drop dough by level tablespoonfuls 2 inches apart onto lightly greased cookie sheets. Bake at 350° for 12 to 15 minutes. Cool slightly on cookie sheets; remove to wire racks. Yield: 5 dozen.

PARTY PIZZAS

    1 pound hot bulk pork sausage
    1 (16-ounce) package process cheese
       spread, diced
  ¼ cup catsup
    2 tablespoons Worcestershire sauce
    1 teaspoon dried whole oregano
    1 teaspoon fennel seeds
    2 (8-ounce) loaves sliced party rye
       bread

Cook sausage until browned in a large skillet, stirring to crumble; drain well. Add remaining ingredients except bread; cook until cheese melts. Spread meat mixture evenly on bread slices; place on ungreased baking sheets. Bake at 350° for 10 minutes or until bubbly. Yield: about 6 dozen.

Note: Party Pizzas may be made ahead and frozen. Place unbaked pizzas in a single layer on large baking sheets; freeze. When slices are frozen, place in plastic bags and store in freezer until needed. To serve, thaw and bake as directed above.

Christmas Journal

As first frost crystallizes the earth and sunset slips in earlier each day, our inner hourglasses whisper that the holidays approach. It's time to take pen in hand and begin planning for the days ahead.

This journal will help you set it all down: the festive events, the loving tasks, the personal traditions that give your holidays meaning.

In *A Christmas Memory*, Truman Capote remembers one such tradition involving a childhood companion and distant cousin: "It's always the same: a morning arrives in November, and my friend, as though officially inaugurating the Christmas time of year that exhilarates her imagination and fuels the blaze of her heart, announces: 'It's fruitcake weather! Fetch our buggy. Help me find my hat.' "

As the days pass, small things contribute to the anticipation — a card from a far away friend, a treasured decoration carefully placed, strains of a favorite carol, aromas from the kitchen.

The challenge is to strike a careful balance between seeing to myriad duties and stopping to absorb the beauty and rarity of the season.

On the following pages, you'll find help in the form of mailing information, card and gift lists, size charts, and a holiday calendar. A party-planning section guides your way to gracious entertaining.

Let this journal ease the task of organization, allowing you time to breathe deeply, light the candles, and savor the season. When days grow long again, leaf through these pages to bring back the essence of Christmas.

Mailing

CARDS

Keep in mind the following U.S. Postal regulations. Envelopes must be rectangular in shape. Envelopes smaller than 3½″ × 5″ cannot be mailed. Envelopes larger than 6⅛″ × 11½″, even if they weigh less than 1 ounce, require extra postage.

PACKAGES

Before you wrap a package, consider the contents, the sturdiness of the box, the cushioning, and closure with tape.

Choose a sturdy box. Include adequate cushioning. Place your return address and address of the recipient inside the box. Wrap the package in brown paper. Use a filament tape. Masking tape, cellophane tape and surgical tape are just not strong enough. Address clearly.

Packages may be sent through the U.S. Postal Service by parcel post in weights up to 70 pounds and measurements of 108″ of combined length and girth.

United Parcel Service (UPS) accepts packages up to 50 pounds for delivery in state, 70 pounds in interstate shipment, and up to 108″ in combined length and girth. There is a pick-up fee for door-to-door service.

CATEGORY	EXAMPLES	CONTAINER	CUSHIONING	CLOSURE
Soft Goods		Self-supporting box or tear-resistant bag		Reinforced tape or sealed bag
Liquids		Leak proof interior and secondary containers	Absorbent	Sealed with filament tape
Powders		Must be sift-proof		Sealed with filament tape
Perishables		Impermeable to content odor	Absorbent	Sealed with filament tape
Fragile Items		Fiberboard (minimum 175 lb test)	To distribute shocks and separate from container surfaces with foamed plastic or padding	Sealed and reinforced with filament tape
Awkward Loads		Fiberboard tubes and boxes with length not over 10 times girth	Pre-formed fiberboard or foamed plastic shapes	Tube ends equal to side wall strength

CONTAINER

Fiberboard

Manufacturer's Certificate
125 lb test to 20 lbs
175 lb test to 40 lbs
275 lb test to 70 lbs

Paperboard up to 10 lbs

CUSHIONING

Wrap each item individually with enough padding to prevent damage from shock

Separate wrapped items from outer package surfaces with padding or foamed plastic

CLOSURE

Pressure Sensitive Filament Tape is preferable to prevent accidental opening

Reinforced Kraft Paper Tape

Kraft Paper Tape

ADDRESSING

Address Labels should be readable from 30″ away and should not be easily smeared or washed off

Should contain ZIP Code

Return Address should also be included inside of carton

Adapted from a U.S. Postal Service poster.

Gifts & Wishes

GIFTS & WISHES (CONTINUED)

Size Charts

Name		Name	
height	weight	height	weight
coat	slacks	coat	slacks
dress	pajamas	dress	pajamas
suit	bathrobe	suit	bathrobe
sweater	shoes	sweater	shoes
shirt	hat	shirt	hat
blouse	gloves	blouse	gloves
skirt	ring	skirt	ring

Name		Name	
height	weight	height	weight
coat	slacks	coat	slacks
dress	pajamas	dress	pajamas
suit	bathrobe	suit	bathrobe
sweater	shoes	sweater	shoes
shirt	hat	shirt	hat
blouse	gloves	blouse	gloves
skirt	ring	skirt	ring

Name		Name	
height	weight	height	weight
coat	slacks	coat	slacks
dress	pajamas	dress	pajamas
suit	bathrobe	suit	bathrobe
sweater	shoes	sweater	shoes
shirt	hat	shirt	hat
blouse	gloves	blouse	gloves
skirt	ring	skirt	ring

Name		Name	
height	weight	height	weight
coat	slacks	coat	slacks
dress	pajamas	dress	pajamas
suit	bathrobe	suit	bathrobe
sweater	shoes	sweater	shoes
shirt	hat	shirt	hat
blouse	gloves	blouse	gloves
skirt	ring	skirt	ring

Christmas Card List

CHRISTMAS CARD LIST (CONTINUED)

_____   _____

_____   _____

_____   _____

_____   _____

_____   _____

_____   _____

_____   _____

_____   _____

_____   _____

_____   _____

_____   _____

_____   _____

_____   _____

_____   _____

_____   _____

_____   _____

_____   _____

_____   _____

_____   _____

Holiday Calendar

Don't worry about organization this year. Keep up with the brisk and busy days before Christmas by jotting it all down here: when company will arrive, which days you'll go on shopping excursions, and which nights you'll dress up and celebrate.

There are school or office occasions to schedule, tree trimmings, Christmas card mailings, all the seasonal events—religious and social—you and your family will want to attend. Writing down major activities will let you see when the crunch might occur and allow you to develop a counterplan.

And by recording your holiday goings-on, then adding your impressions after the fact, you'll be creating a diary to cherish. You can even slip snapshots between these pages to help keep the memories fresh.

Not only will you enjoy reliving the special moments that made Christmas 1985 unique, you'll also be able to use this calendar in coming years to head off problems in scheduling and to recall tricks that worked.

Friday, November 1

Saturday, November 2

Sunday, November 3

Monday, November 4

Tuesday, November 5

Wednesday, November 6

Thursday, November 7

Friday, November 8

Saturday, November 9

Sunday, November 10

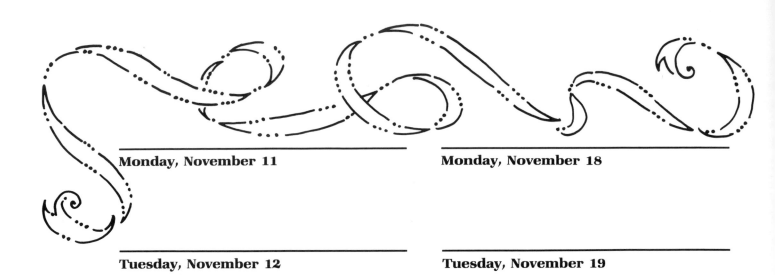

Monday, November 11

Monday, November 18

Tuesday, November 12

Tuesday, November 19

Wednesday, November 13

Wednesday, November 20

Thursday, November 14

Thursday, November 21

Friday, November 15

Friday, November 22

Saturday, November 16

Saturday, November 23

Sunday, November 17

Sunday, November 24

Monday, November 25

Monday, December 2

Tuesday, November 26

Tuesday, December 3

Wednesday, November 27

Wednesday, December 4

Thursday, November 28
Thanksgiving Day

Thursday, December 5

Friday, November 29

Friday, December 6

Saturday, November 30

Saturday, December 7

Sunday, December 1

Sunday, December 8

Monday, December 9

Monday, December 16

Tuesday, December 10

Tuesday, December 17

Wednesday, December 11

Wednesday, December 18

Thursday, December 12

Thursday, December 19

Friday, December 13

Friday, December 20

Saturday, December 14

Saturday, December 21

Sunday, December 15

Sunday, December 22

Monday, December 23

Monday, December 30

Tuesday, December 24

Tuesday, December 31

Wednesday, December 25
Christmas Day

Wednesday, January 1
New Year's Day

Thursday, December 26

Friday, December 27

Saturday, December 28

Sunday, December 29

Party Planning

Home is where Christmas happens. And with the centuries-old tradition of entertaining, we extend our personal greetings to those close to us.

There are many ways to entertain during the long holiday season—cocktail parties, a traditional Christmas Eve supper for close friends, and even cooperative get-togethers. But if you plan to tackle only one holiday event, a buffet party is ideal for this time of year.

A buffet can be planned and completed without too much confusion, making your home a warm and welcoming spot during this season of hustle and bustle.

So if you're going to open your home for the holidays this year, follow these tips on mixing Southern warmth and hospitality. Each one is designed to help you accomplish party tasks as easily as possible while you spread the Christmas spirit.

Getting Things Underway

Since planning is the secret to staging a successful party, holiday entertaining begins with planning. Keep an organization book with notes on preparing the menu, making table and furniture arrangements, and other details. (A plain loose-leaf notebook will do.)

At least four weeks before your party, plan the guest list and mail invitations. Note when local churches, clubs, schools, or friends are having their big events, so that your party will not conflict. By sending your invitations out early, you will get a good place on the calendar.

When drawing up the guest list, select people who will really enjoy being together; this is not a time to reciprocate dinner favors. To write your invitations, you might try a calligraphy pen. A special pen can make your handwriting fancier and more interesting. Don't hesitate to put an RSVP on the invitation, including a date by which you'd like guests to respond. If your invitation list is large, and your house small, you might stagger the hours in the invitations so that guests won't all arrive at the same time.

After the invitations are sent, make two timetables: On the first, list those things that need to be done ahead; on the second, jot down tasks that must be done the day of the party. You might also divide your grocery and liquor lists into items that can be purchased ahead of time—such as flours, extracts, and candied fruits—and perishables, which must be bought close to the time of the party.

Many party supplies, such as matches, candles, and paper napkins, can be bought over a period of time during regular trips to the supermarket. (Buy candles early, to make sure you get the right colors and sizes.) Stock up gradually on carbonated beverages, liquor, and staples that are too heavy to carry home on one trip. And remember that some liquor stores still deliver.

Other details to take care of ahead of time include ordering special flowers or plants, looking into the rental of extra china, glassware, or flatware you'll need (for delivery the day before the party), and polishing the silver and brass. Tie the latter in tarnish-preventive silver cloths, available in department stores, after polishing; then label so that you'll know the contents.

This is also the time to consider getting help for your party—to serve, babysit, or assist with clean-up. Ask friends if they can suggest someone reliable, check with the vocational office of a nearby college, call your local high school, or ask around the neighborhood for a reliable teenager eager to earn some spending money.

Prepare everything you can in advance, like meat dishes, bread, and dough for rolls and desserts. And let the rest of your family in on the fun, allowing them to choose what they'd like to do. Children, for example, can get out all the Christmas records and arrange them in a brightly colored basket by the stereo, to make sure the house is filled with the sounds of Christmas all season.

Setting the Mood

Little touches create a memorable mood at Christmas. For delicate lighting, use pink light bulbs, or pleasantly scented votive candles. Set one candle out alone to call attention to a special spot, line several up on a hutch, or set them in sherbet glasses arranged on a silver tray. The heat of the candles should not harm the containers, but pouring a little water in the glasses first lessens the chance of breakage. If some wax does stick, use a bit of hot water to release it.

Music and celebrations are also natural companions. Background music should be playing as the first guests arrive, since they will be standing alone in an area prepared for a larger group. But turn off the music when the party really gets started.

Inside, plan to keep the temperature cooler than usual. (If winter in the South is unusually warm, you may even consider turning on the air-conditioning, as did the Georgia couple featured on page 22.) And outside, you'll want to present some kind of festive greeting for guests—a wreath made of materials from your own region, tiny white lights twinkling in the trees, or a lush bouquet of ribbons and greenery tied to the mailbox.

Decking the Halls

Holiday decorating should give guests a warm welcome the minute they walk through the door. Arrangements can be as uncomplicated as a cluster of greenery, a bowl of shiny ornaments, or bunches of baby's breath tucked into the Christmas tree. Just keep decorations simple and personal, and try to have them in place a day or two before you entertain.

Much of the South is blessed with flowers at any season, so we're not limited to the traditional Christmas greens. Camellias, hibiscus, and roses can be used in low arrangements or centerpieces. And other flowering plants ready to brighten a holiday table or window include azaleas forced into early bloom; the Jerusalem cherry plant with its dark-green foliage and red fruit; fanciful florist's cyclamen; and kalanchoes, with their star-shaped blossoms in neon-like shades of red, pink, yellow, and orange.

Rosemary and lavender, interspersed with evergreen, make a nice herbal arrangement. (The story goes that Mary draped the Christ Child's freshly washed linens over these two plants to dry.) But don't forget the plants native to your own area. Marsh lavender, heather, and Texas broomweed, as well as cabbage palm fronds, can all be used for regional Christmas decorating.

Of course, the traditional poinsettia always adds a fresh touch to the season. Select the plant with the most branches. It should have healthy, dark-green foliage all the way down the stems, and flowers should be closed or only beginning to open. (For more on poinsettias, see "Christmas at Callaway Gardens," page 4.)

Make a centerpiece of pixie poinsettias by removing the plants from their pots, wrapping the roots in small plastic bags, and placing them in clear vases filled with Spanish moss (available from florist's shops). Or place cut poinsettias in a clear container filled with glass marbles, for a simple yet elegant effect. (To prepare cut poinsettias for use, first seal the stems by cutting each end cleanly with a sharp knife and passing the stem through a candle flame—just enough to singe the end.)

Magnolia leaves are handsome in holiday arrangements. To keep the leaves flexible, condition them in a glycerine solution, as follows. Take cuttings of the branches and, at the end of each stem, make a couple of 3-inch-long cuts lengthwise. Then place branches in a large container filled with a mixture of three parts water to one part glycerine. Keep adding the mixture as it evaporates. After about two months, leaves should be a consistent, rich brown color. Gather them into a large basket by the fireplace, mix them with fresh evergreen on a sideboard or in an entry hall, or spray-paint some leaves gold for a striking effect.

For table decorations, consider using vintage linens with satin ribbon and plaid runners, an antique-looking toy sleigh arranged with other old toys, or hurricane shades filled with colored ornaments. Dress up serving trays with small dolls and Christmas trees, or the whole top of a pineapple, dotted with cranberries.

And, finally, somewhere in the house, hang some mistletoe so that guests can exchange a kiss. Mistletoe symbolizes the promise of spring and the return of peace—the perfect Christmas party spirit.

Keeping Things Moving

Let the entire house entertain your guests by placing food stations so that the group is motivated to move easily from room to room. Serving food in every room cuts congestion in the dining area, and allows guests to snack without feeling they have made too many trips to the buffet table.

To set up food in other rooms, use the furniture that's already there. Serve coffee or cider on a table in the hallway. Let an old armoire become a bar. Or use a fancy writing desk for desserts. If you need more furniture for serving, bring in moveable carts or folding tables. Just be sure to protect the surface of your furniture from moisture, heat, or scratches by placing a plastic place mat or tablecloth under pretty fabric coverings. Use cloths in a holiday print just for Christmas, or in a red polka-dot pattern that can be used again for Valentine's Day and Fourth of July reunions.

If you decide to arrange your buffet on the dining table, you'll want to organize things so that guests can serve themselves from either side. For convenience, plates can be placed where the line begins; napkins and flatware go at the end.

It also helps to separate the wine and non-alcoholic beverage tables from the bar, usually placing them on opposite sides of the room. Wine glasses can be filled in advance, and extra bottles in buckets will add an aesthetic touch to the table arrangement.

But the biggest advantage to this system is that it speeds up traffic at the bar.

When you have the design of your party well in mind, you might try walking through the house, taking inventory of available tables, and deciding where extra chairs might be placed. Make sure you have a place for everyone to sit, or at least room in which they can stand and mingle comfortably.

Planning a Menu That's Easy on You

It's fun to introduce a new food at a party, or find a different way to present a familiar dish, especially as an alternative to foods served often at this time of year. But don't make your menu complicated or demanding. Avoid dishes, such as souffles, that require a lot of last-minute preparation, and concentrate on things like casseroles that are easy to make and keep heated.

Since most guests at your party will be juggling a drink, plate, napkin, and fork, no dish at the buffet should be hard to handle. Avoid crumbly bread, flaky crusts, sauces, and foods that need spices or condiments. Drippy sauces can be a disaster for guests in evening dress!

Start with the kind of dishes that may look elaborate, but can be made in advance and chilled until party time. Take advantage of commercially prepared foods, such as sliced beef and breads from a deli. For emergency refills on hors d'oeuvres, use cheese (either in block or spread form); or items in jars and cans, like olives, smoked oysters, and artichoke hearts. (When you're deciding on the amount of food you'll need, remember that for a midnight buffet, you can reduce your normal food supply by about ten percent.)

On the big day, set up the bar and the coffee service, place flowers where you want them, and take care of last-minute details like filling nut dishes and putting out extra ashtrays and coasters. Portable toasters will expand your oven space, and an insulated ice chest will come in handy for keeping beverages and other items cold.

Patterns

Reflections of Home

Directions on page 64
Full-size patterns

For scalloped roof design, do not punch.
Draw from back with ballpoint pen.

Punch hole
for hanging.

For latticed roof design,
do not punch.
Draw from back
with ballpoint pen.
Punch hole for hanging.

Punch hole
for hanging.

137

A Rag Doll with Country Style

Directions on page 66
Full-size patterns
Add ¼″ seam allowances.
Patterns continue on pages 140-141.

Leave open.

Apron bodice back
Cut 4 from muslin.

Center back

Leg
Cut 4 from muslin.

Apron bodice front
Cut 2 from muslin.

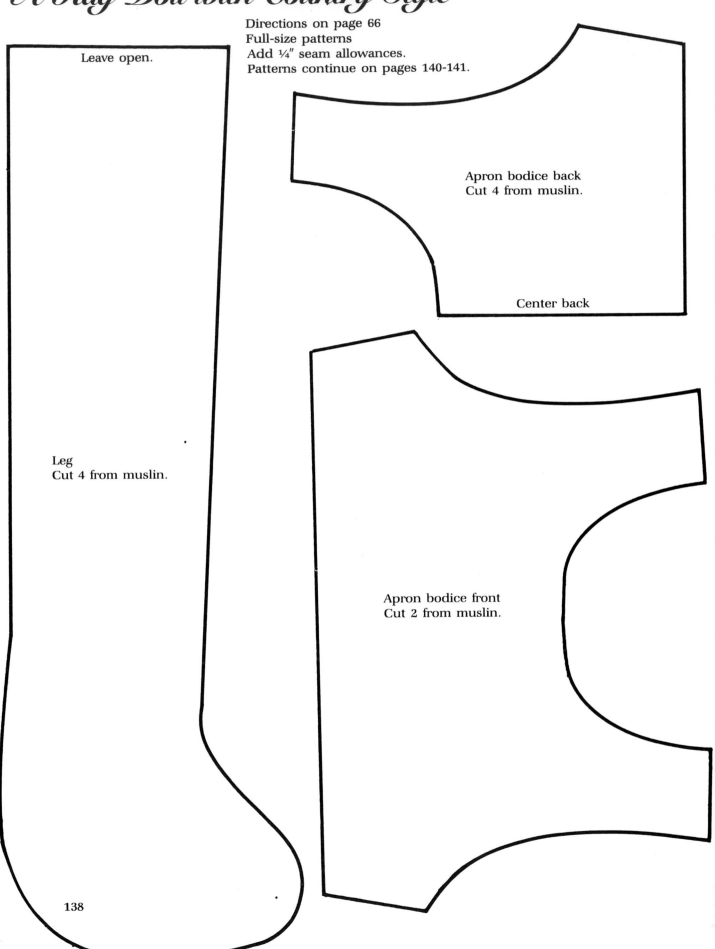

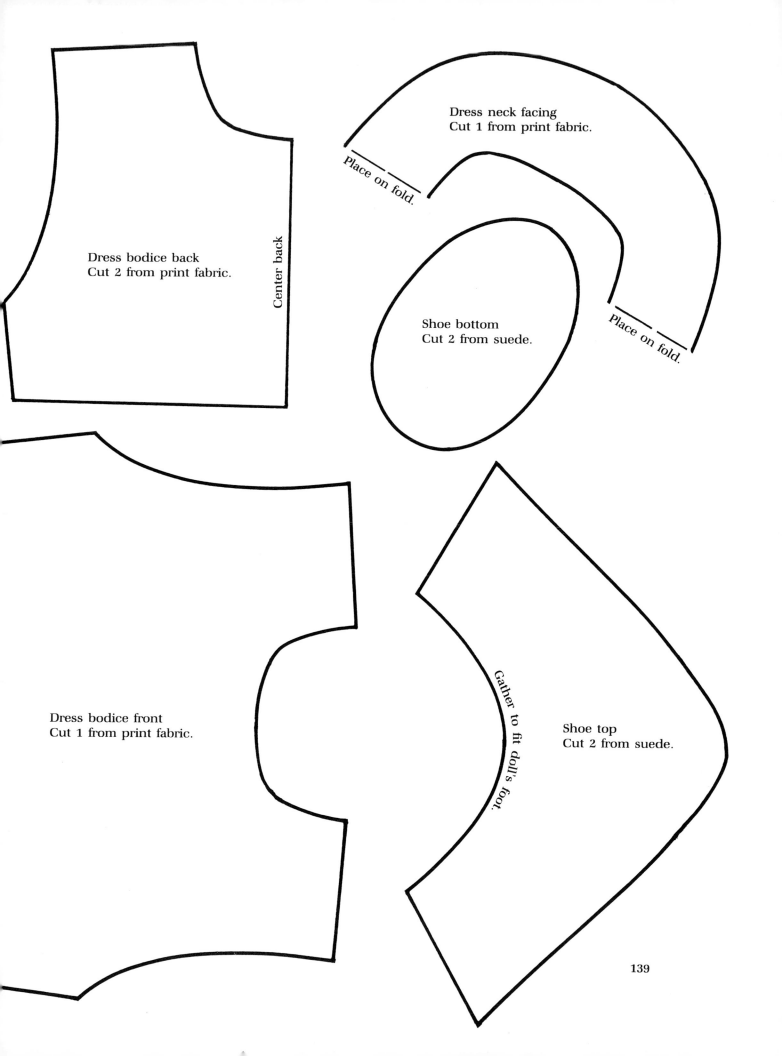

Dress bodice back
Cut 2 from print fabric.

Center back

Dress neck facing
Cut 1 from print fabric.

Place on fold.

Place on fold.

Shoe bottom
Cut 2 from suede.

Dress bodice front
Cut 1 from print fabric.

Gather to fit doll's foot.

Shoe top
Cut 2 from suede.

139

Continued

Match squares and continue pattern
opposite page.

Paint eyes
and nose
medium brown.

Paint cheeks
light brown
with soft edges.

Match X's and continue pattern on opposite
page.

Doll body
Cut 2 from muslin.

Match cir
and conti
on opposite p

½ of pattern (Reverse for other half or place on fold.)

140

Extend 2″.

Extend 2″.

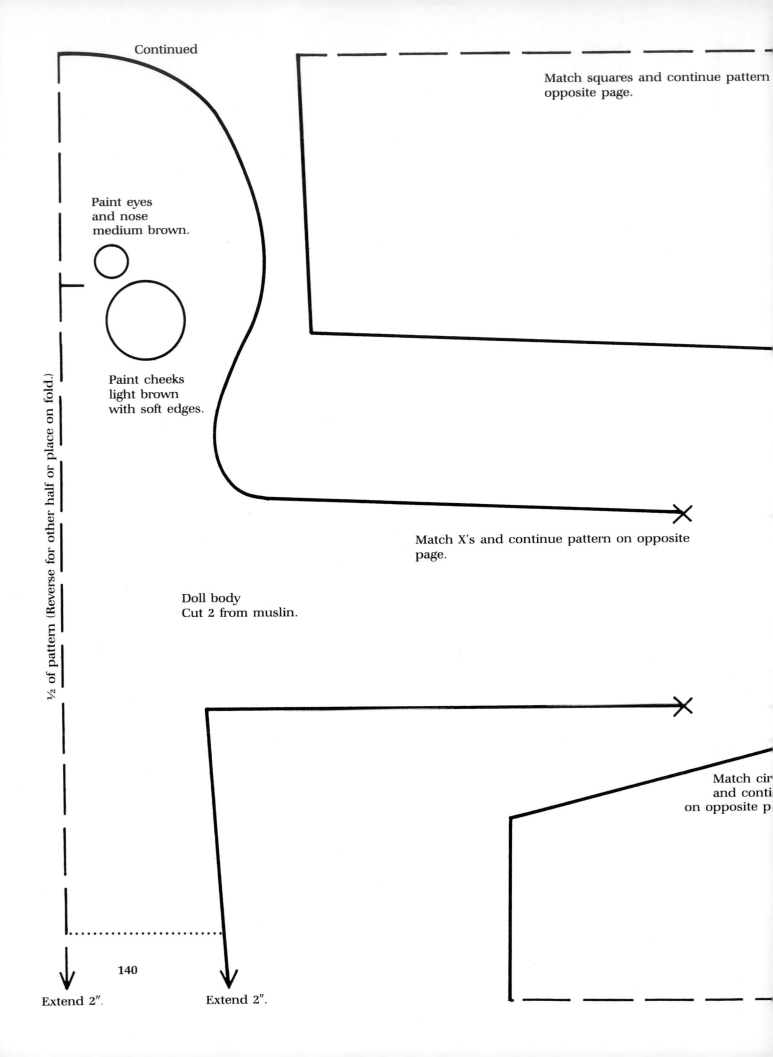

Bloomers
Cut 2 from muslin.

Fold under here↑
and stitch
to form casing
for elastic.

A Rag Doll
with Country Style

Directions on page 66
Full-size patterns
Add ¼" seam allowances.
Additional pattern pieces:
Dimensions include ¼" seam allowances.

Gather along this line.

Dress sleeve
Cut 2 from print fabric.

141

Net-Darn a Holiday Backdrop

Directions on page 56

142

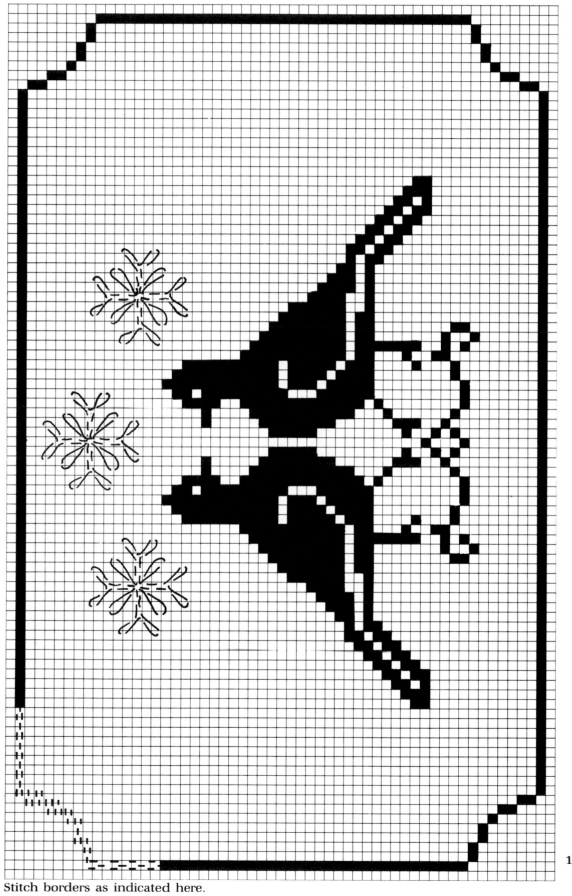

Stitch borders as indicated here.

143

Nightshirt Santa

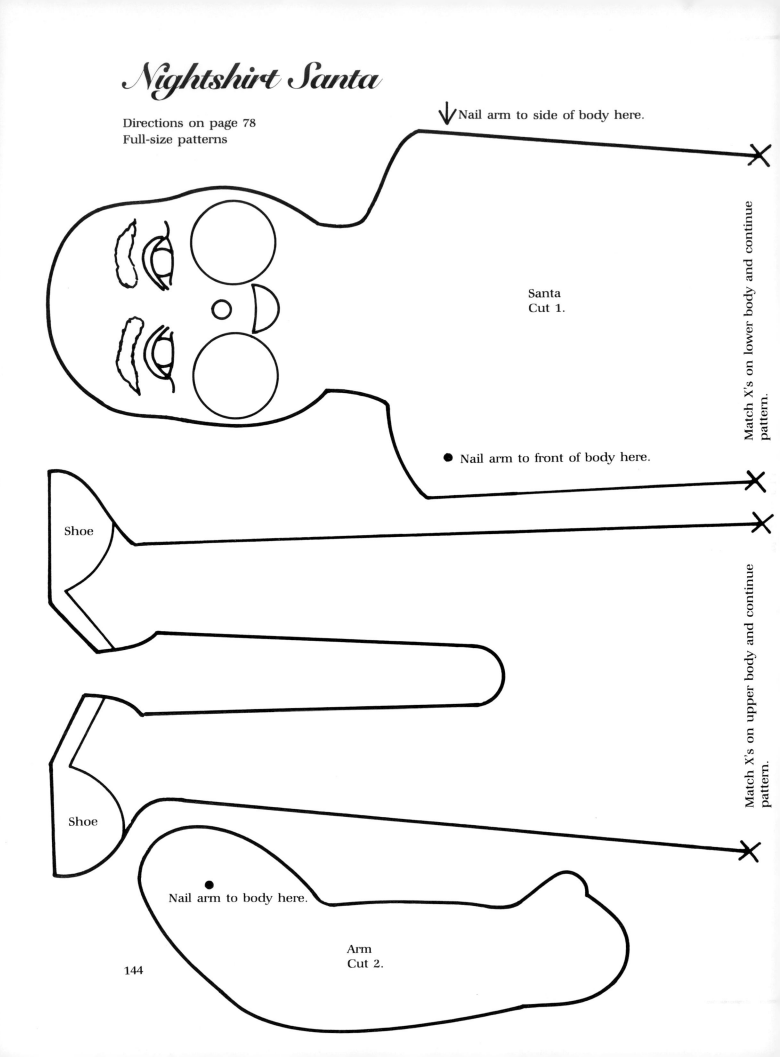

Directions on page 78
Full-size patterns

↓Nail arm to side of body here.

Match X's on lower body and continue pattern.

Santa
Cut 1.

● Nail arm to front of body here.

Shoe

Match X's on upper body and continue pattern.

Shoe

● Nail arm to body here.

Arm
Cut 2.

144

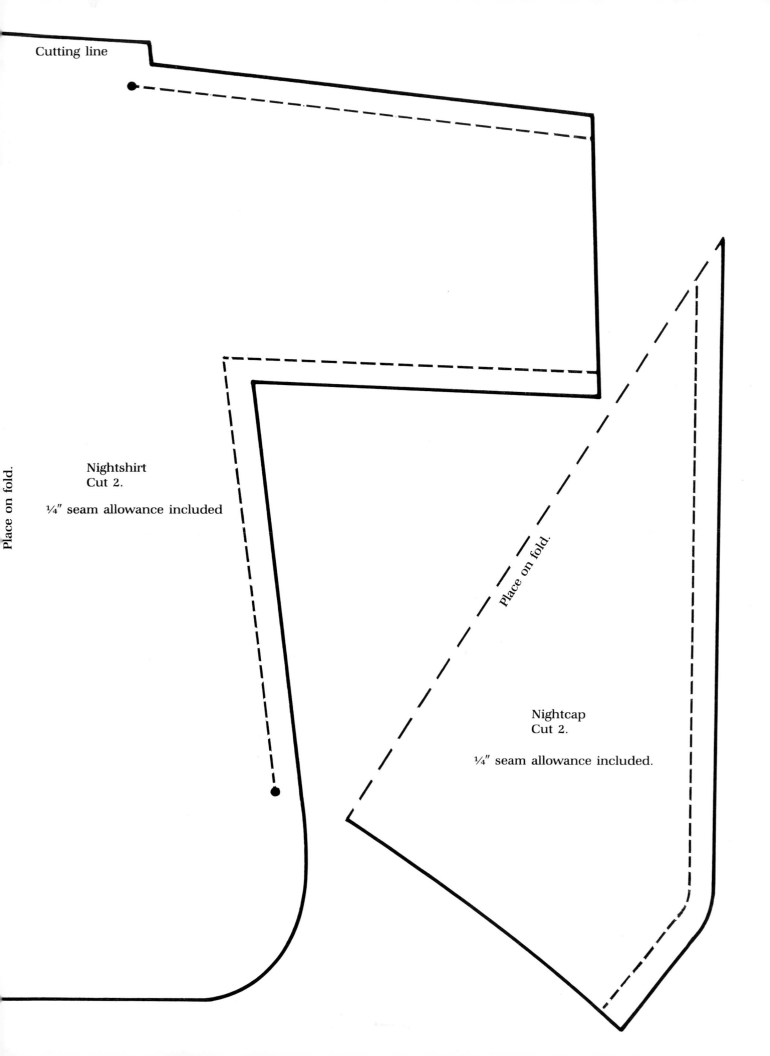

Cutting line

Place on fold.

Nightshirt
Cut 2.

¼″ seam allowance included

Place on fold.

Nightcap
Cut 2.

¼″ seam allowance included.

Say Welcome with Cross-Stitch

Directions on page 82

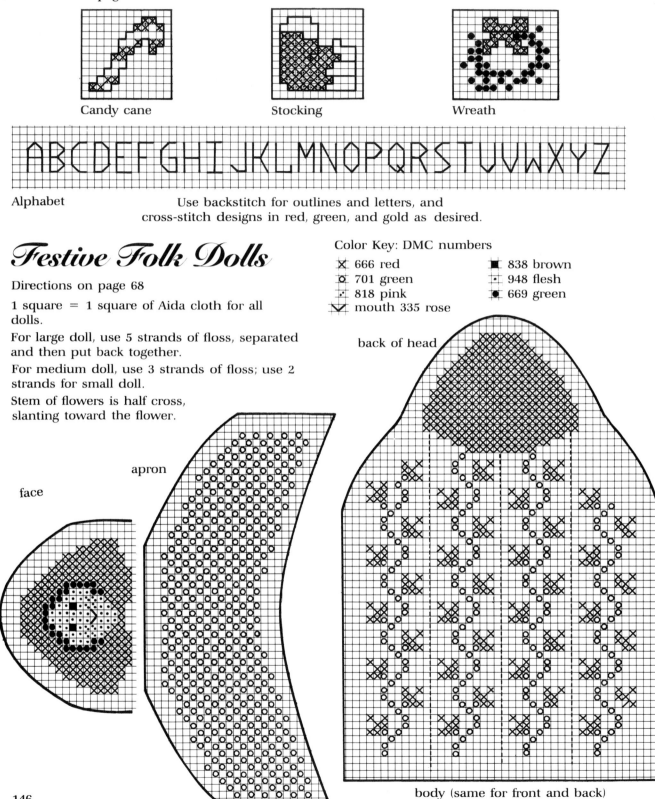

Candy cane

Stocking

Wreath

Alphabet

ABCDEFGHIJKLMNOPQRSTUVWXYZ

Use backstitch for outlines and letters, and
cross-stitch designs in red, green, and gold as desired.

Festive Folk Dolls

Directions on page 68

1 square = 1 square of Aida cloth for all
dolls.

For large doll, use 5 strands of floss, separated
and then put back together.

For medium doll, use 3 strands of floss; use 2
strands for small doll.

Stem of flowers is half cross,
slanting toward the flower.

Color Key: DMC numbers

X 666 red   ■ 838 brown
o 701 green   ⋮ 948 flesh
⋮ 818 pink   ● 669 green
∨ mouth 335 rose

back of head

apron

face

body (same for front and back)

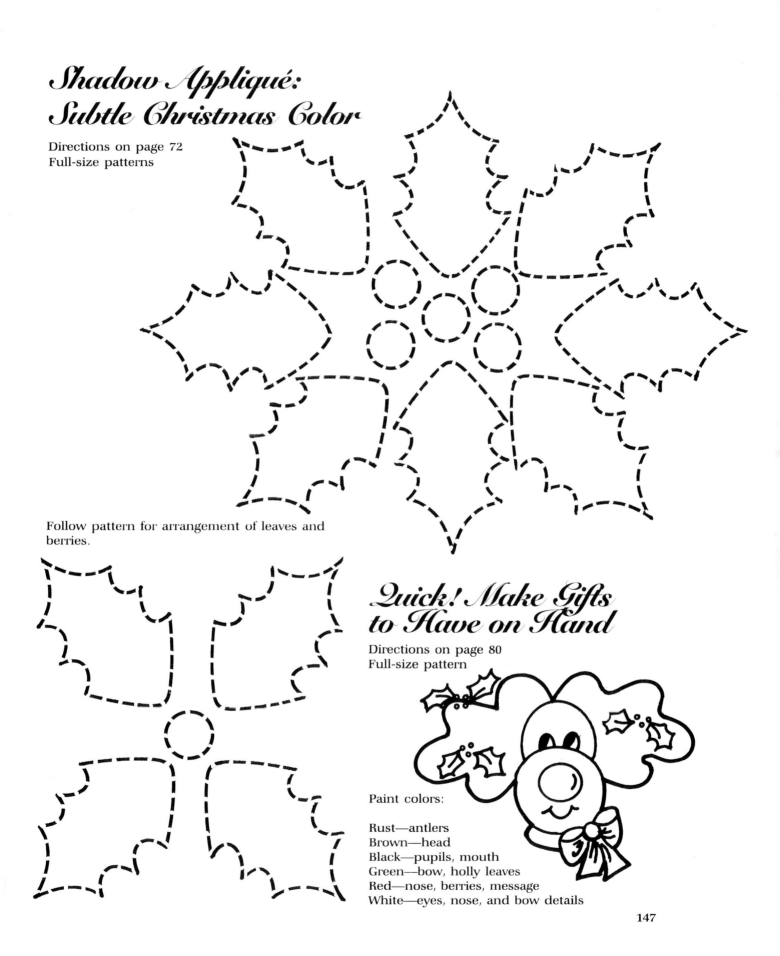

Shadow Appliqué: Subtle Christmas Color

Directions on page 72
Full-size patterns

Follow pattern for arrangement of leaves and berries.

Quick! Make Gifts to Have on Hand

Directions on page 80
Full-size pattern

Paint colors:

Rust—antlers
Brown—head
Black—pupils, mouth
Green—bow, holly leaves
Red—nose, berries, message
White—eyes, nose, and bow details

Featherweight Angel

Directions on page 54
Full-size pattern

Country Gift Baskets

Directions on page 44.
Full-size patterns

Lacy Collars from Old Linens

Directions on page 59
Full-size pattern

Front neckline

1"

Back neckline

This pattern is sized for an average adult.
Adjust width and depth of opening according
to size of person who will wear it.

Fold line

Scents for Your Kitchen

Directions on page 43
Full-size pattern

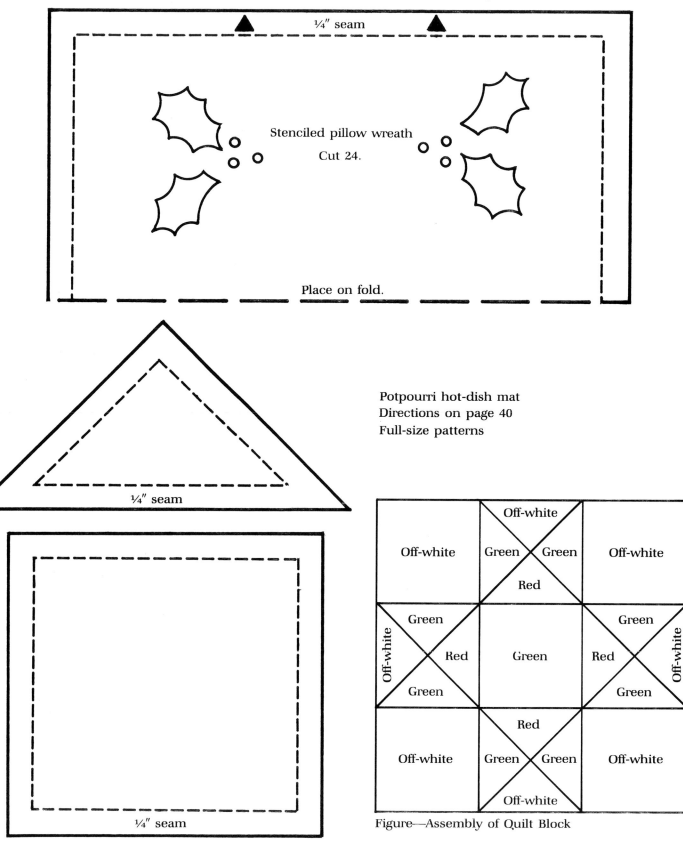

▲ ¼" seam ▲

Stenciled pillow wreath
Cut 24.

Place on fold.

¼" seam

Potpourri hot-dish mat
Directions on page 40
Full-size patterns

¼" seam

Off-white	Off-white Green Green Red	Off-white
Off-white	Green Red Green Red Green	Green Red Green
Off-white	Red Green Green Off-white	Off-white

Figure—Assembly of Quilt Block

Ribbon Rays Make a Heavenly Angel

Directions on page 63
Full-size pattern

For sequence of attaching ribbon, follow numbers in sections with bold outlines.

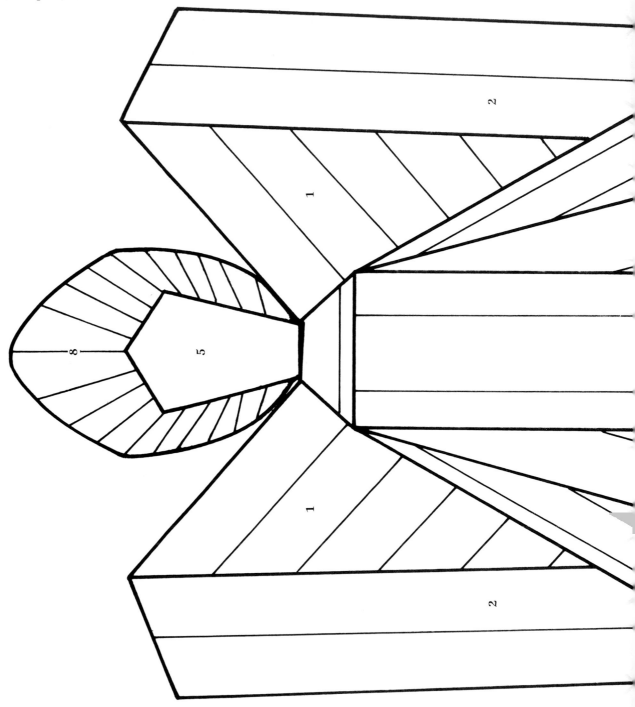

Match X's and continue pattern across the page.

Match X's and continue pattern across the
page.

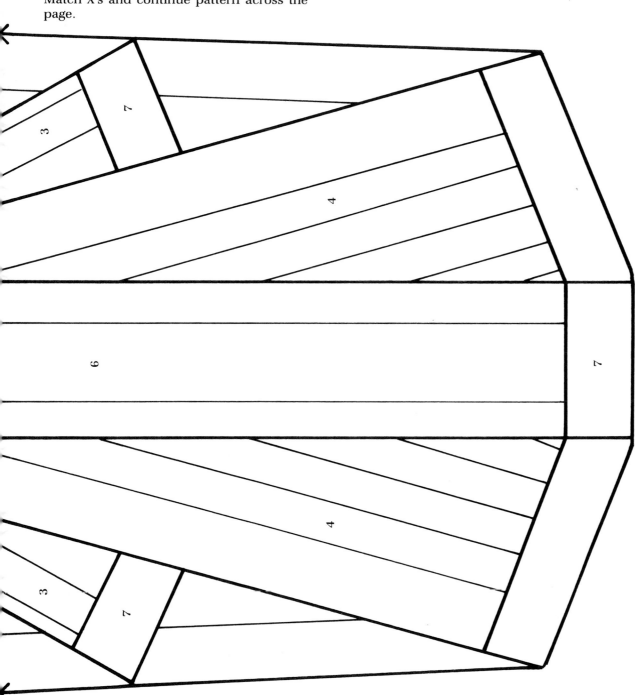

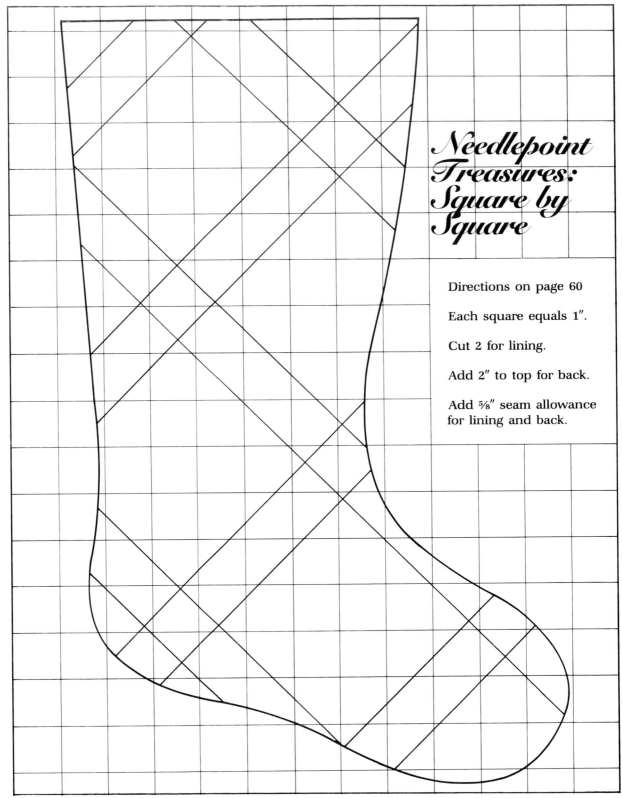

Needlepoint Treasures: Square by Square

Directions on page 60

Each square equals 1".

Cut 2 for lining.

Add 2" to top for back.

Add ⅝" seam allowance for lining and back.

Transfer outline and lattice pattern to canvas. Use charts for designs in squares and pick up background patterns from charts for partial squares. Work lattice outline in dark coral and poinsettias from chart, using continental stitch for both. Lattice background is white and done in basketweave stitch. Straight lines and small areas of designs in squares are worked in continental stitch. Use basketweave stitch for large areas of design, and use mosaic stitch for white part of tablecloths and green part of wallpaper.

Color Key (for stocking):

#3 pearl cotton   embroidery floss (do not separate)

DMC Numbers	Skeins
X 349 dk. coral	2
‖ 726 lt. topaz	2
= 703 chartreuse	2
• 518 lt. wedgewood	3
∕ 3328 salmon	1
⊙ 3345 hunter green	1
v 3347 yellow green	1
☐ white	14

DMC Numbers
◢ 918 dk. red copper
⊻ 920 med. copper
⟍ 318 lt. steel grey
⊙ 676 lt. old gold
● 680 dk. old gold
■ black

} 1 skein each color

For ornaments, check chart for colors. Use 1 skein of each.

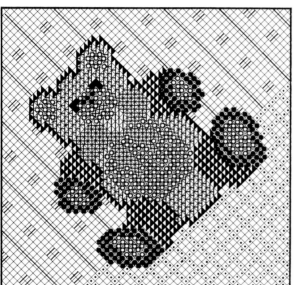

A Deer Mailbox Cover

Directions on page 26

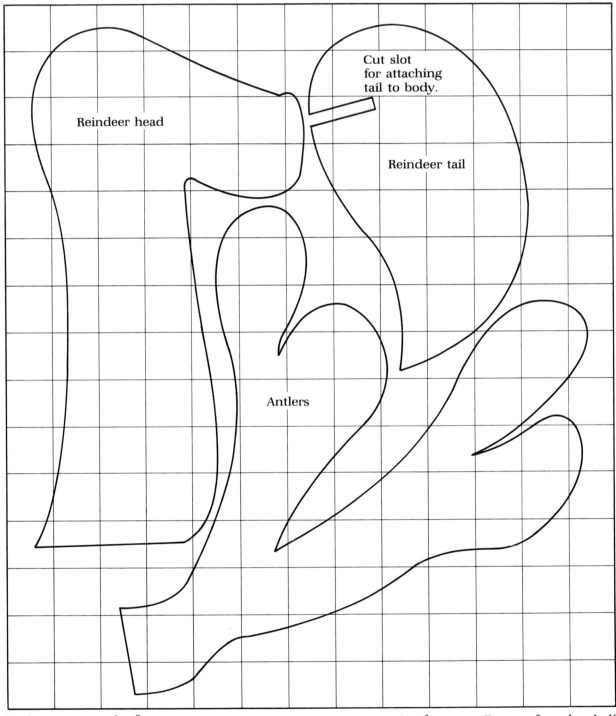

Reindeer head

Cut slot
for attaching
tail to body.

Reindeer tail

Antlers

Each square equals 1″.

½ of pattern. Reverse for other half.

154

Contributors

Special thanks to John Floyd, senior horti-
culturist, and Linda Askey, associate garden
editor, at *Southern Living*, and to the *Southern Living* Test Kitchens staff. Thanks also to
Christine Davis, needlework consultant.

DESIGNERS
Bettye Ann Achorn
    holly days carafe....................................81
Cynthia Deborah Bogart
    reindeer mailbox cover..........................26
    stenciled gift baskets.............................44
Andrea Bush
    lacy collars...58
Carolin Caverly
    folk dolls...68
Virginia Chaney
    cookies and dolls....................................48
Karen Clenney
    glittering candle holders.......................34
Sally Downing
    tree with toys..48
Laura A. Frazure
    nightshirt Santa......................................78
Jan Garrett
    ruffled hearth basket.............................74
    cross-stitch guest towels.......................82
Martha Haarbauer
    ribbon plaids...36
    ribbon angel..62
Cynthia F. Hatchett
    magnolia leaf wreath..............................30
Dora Hooks
    hydrangea wreath...................................29
Diana L. Judson
    featherweight angel................................54
Cissy Kay
    net-darned hanging................................56
Pete Kilgo
    reindeer mailbox cover..........................26
Ellen M. Maxwell
    potpourri hot-dish mat...........................40
    potpourri pillow wreath..........................42
Bonnie L. Mullock
    country rag doll.......................................66
    nightshirt Santa......................................78

Janet Oberliessen
    wreath with ark and animals.................50
    cupboard with cards, dolls....................52
Rosalie Peters
    needlepoint treasures.............................60
Dolly Thompson
    flower arrangement.................................47
Carol M. Tipton
    pom-pom sweaters...................................70
    ribbon-laced afghan................................76
Gary Lynn Trentham
    natural wreath...28
Jo Voce
    nandina berry wreath.............................31
    cinnamon stick ornaments.....................40
    spiced apple wreath................................43
    jar lid toppers...80
    burlap bag wrap......................................81
Carol L. Wagner
    shadow appliqué set................................72
Michael Walls
    garlands...38
Jan Way
    punched-copper ornaments....................64

PHOTOGRAPHERS
Katherine Adams
    8, 9, 10, 11, 12, 13, 30, 32, 33, 43, 46, 47, 48,
    48-49, 50-51, 52, 53, 73
Jim Bathie
    27
Gary Clark
    cover, contents, title page, 1, 2-3, 5, 6, 6-7,
    14-15, 16-17, 17, 18, 19, 20, 21, 22, 23, 24, 25,
    34-35, 35, 37, 40, 41, 42, 44, 45, 54, 55, 58, 60,
    61, 62, 63, 64-65, 65, 68-69, 70-71, 72, 74-75, 76,
    77, 78, 79, 80, 82, 83, 123
Beth Maynor
    28, 31, 38, 39
Kim McRae
    57, 66, 81
Courtland W. Richards
    29
Charles E. Walton, IV
    84-85, 86, 89, 91, 92, 95, 98, 101, 103, 104,
    108, 111, 114, 118, 119

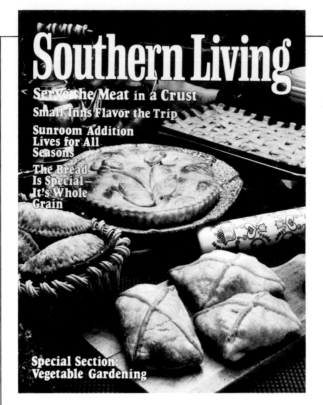